The Oxford Student's Harmony

A PRACTICAL APPROACH TO CREATIVE MUSICIANSHIP

EDWIN SMITH
and
DAVID RENOUF

BOOK TWO

Music Department

OXFORD UNIVERSITY PRESS

44 CONDUIT STREET, LONDON W.1

First published 1966
Second impression 1968
Third impression 1969
Fourth impression 1972
Fifth impression 1973

To the students of Nottingham College of Education

Printed in England by
John Thorpe & Son Ltd. Wembley

CONTENTS

Acknowledgements are due to the following for permission to reproduce extracts from songs or music: Boosey & Hawkes Music Publishers Ltd. (Delius's *Appalachia*, Glazounov's *Theme and Variations*, *Eighteen Shining Buttons* arr. Mátyás Seiber from *Yugoslav Folk-Songs*, Britten's *War Requiem* (excerpts from the poem of Wilfrid Owen by permission of Mr. Harold Owen and Chatto & Windus Ltd.); J. B. Cramer & Co., Ltd. *(The Loyal Lover)*; Curwen Edition *(High Germany* and *Billy Boy)*; Editio Musica, Budapest (Bartók's *Bagatelle)*; The English Folk Dance and Song Society *(The Old Man from Lee, The Gentleman Soldier, The Golden Vanity, Death and the Lady, Farewell my Joy and Heart)*; EFDS Publications Ltd. *(The Tree in the Bog)*; Hinrichsen Edition Ltd., the copyright owners of Peters Edition (Kabalevsky's *Toccata*); Thomas Nelson & Sons Ltd. *(Good King Arthur* from *A First Song Book* by Fosbrooke Allen); Novello & Co., Ltd. *(Spanish Ladies*, Parry's *Laudate Dominum*, Elgar's *Dream of Gerontius*, Bach's *Christmas Oratorio* and *St. John Passion* (English words), *Searching for Lambs, Farewell Nancy*, and *The Cuckoo* from *Some Lesser-known Folk Songs II*, *I will give my love an apple* from *Collected Folk Songs I)*; Schott & Co., Ltd. (Humperdinck's *Hansel and Gretel*, Tippett's *Sonata*, Wagner's *Die Meistersinger* (English translation by Frederick Jameson)); Stainer & Bell Ltd. *(Leave now mine eyes lamenting)*; Ruth L. Tongue *(Christmas Carol from Somerset)*; Ursula Vaughan Williams *(Lovely Joan, Robin Hood and the Pedlar, Come all you wild young people)*; Musikverlag Wilhelm Zimmermann *(A Cossack Lullaby)*; Oxford University Press *(David of the White Rock*, translated by J. P. B. Dobbs, from *Oxford School Music Book Senior Book* 2, *Rocking* and *Pat-a-pan* from *The Oxford Book of Carols)*.

Thanks are also due to the Welsh Joint Education Committee, Joint Matriculation Board, Trinity College of Music, London and the Royal Academy of Music, London, for permission to quote from various examination papers.

CHAPTER ONE

MODES

Sing and harmonize this Yugoslav folk-song. Notice the three-bar rhythm.

You will have discovered that the tonality is not that of F major or D minor. In fact, this is a modal tune, based upon the following scale:

Now sing this spirited arrangement for unaccompanied voices by Mátyás Seiber:

*Eighteen Shining Buttons**

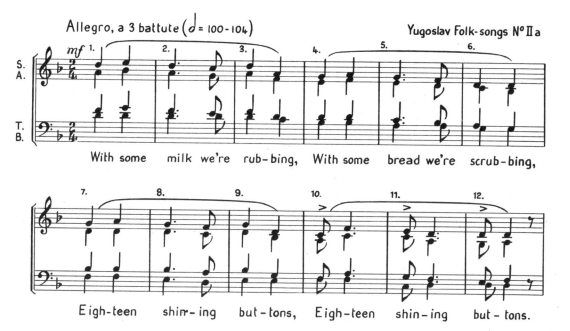

*From *Yugoslav Folk-songs*, copyright 1947 by Boosey & Co. Ltd.

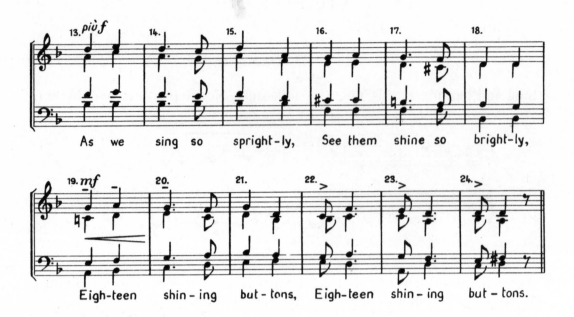

As we sing so spright-ly, See them shine so bright-ly,

Eigh-teen shin-ing but-tons, Eigh-teen shin-ing but-tons.

You will notice that the harmonies in bars 1–12 are derived from the scale we have quoted. More modern harmonies are employed in bars 13–24, but they are in keeping with the character of the tune.

For the past three hundred years or so Western music has been based almost entirely upon the major and minor modes. In earlier times the position was very different; musicians then made use of a greater variety of modes. Some of these have come back into favour in the 20th century and are playing a part in the shaping of our musical language. We need to know something about them if we are to have a proper appreciation of our musical heritage.

A scale ('scala': a ladder), shows a way or 'mode' of dividing an interval into a series of graduated steps. Most commonly the interval to be divided is the octave, and we are all familiar with the eight-note scale where the interval between one note and the next is a tone or semitone.

You will realize that there are a number of ways in which tones and semi-tones may be ordered within the octave. Musicians have explored various possibilities and each distinctive arrangement adopted as a basis for composition is known as a MODE.

Here are some of the modes employed in pre-classical music. There were twelve in all. Of these, five emerged as being more favoured than the rest, namely, the Dorian, Phrygian, Mixolydian, Aeolian, and Ionian modes, and these are the ones you are most likely to meet in 16th-century music and in folk-song.

Dorian   Phrygian

r m f s l t d r   m f s l t d r m

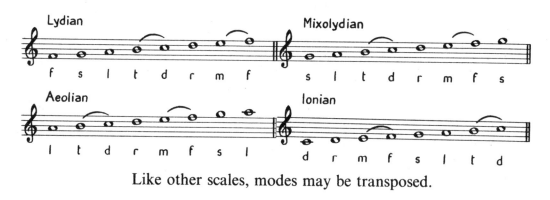

Like other scales, modes may be transposed.

Experiment at the keyboard. Play one octave of the Aeolian mode beginning on each of the following notes in turn: C, G, D, E, and B. Sing the sol-fa names as you play, and afterwards write out the scales putting in the appropriate key signatures.

Many of our most beautiful folk melodies are modal. Do not make the mistake of thinking that because they make a simple and direct appeal that they are therefore necessarily lacking in artistry and subtlety. Remember that the aim of art is to conceal art. There is much we can learn from the finest of these melodies. Let us examine a number of Aeolian and Dorian tunes from the point of view of their melodic and rhythmic structure. They are tunes that you should know well. Learn them by heart and relish their modal flavour. They will make their best effect when sung unaccompanied.

Searching for Lambs

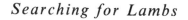

In 'Searching for Lambs' we have a fine example of a tune that grows out of an opening idea as a plant grows from a seed. What a shapely opening phrase this is, with its gentle rise and fall, and its easy, unrestricted flow. We are carried away to the open fields and the calm of the countryside.

The opening two-bar phrase is answered by an imitative phrase of similar length, and these in turn are balanced by a long, unbroken phrase of four bars. The tune achieves unity by the repetition of one melodic idea and yet there is no hint of rigidity because of the artistry of the rhythm.

Here is a verse of poetry that might well be set to music in a similar manner:

> She is so proper and so pure,
> Full stedfast, stabill and demure,
> There is none such, ye may be sure,
> As my swete swetyng.

Write in the Aeolian mode. Here is an opening you might care to adopt:

High Germany

In 'High Germany' we observe a different structure. Here is a tune with four phrases of equal length and an ABBA pattern. But notice that although the A and B phrases are contrasted, they are by no means unrelated. Certain rhythmic and melodic motifs occur throughout the tune giving it unity in variety. Like a sermon that keeps to the text, this tune sticks to the point, and the recurring motifs give it the quality of inevitability and make it memorable. Here are some of the motifs concerned:

Bearing these points in mind, compose a marching song in the Aeolian mode, adopting an ABBA form. Here are some suggested openings:

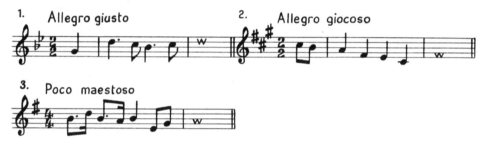

Farewell Nancy

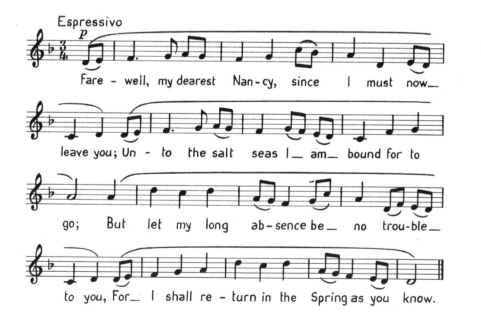

Fare - well, my dearest Nan-cy, since I must now— leave you; Un - to the salt seas I— am— bound for to go; But let my long ab-sence be— no trou-ble— to you, For— I shall re - turn in the Spring as you know.

The melody of 'Farewell Nancy' is most beautifully contrived. Again we find four phrases of equal length. The last three phrases are variants of the opening statement. All four phrases have characteristics in common, yet no two are quite alike. The crotchets at the beginning of the third phrase are a wonderful inspiration, providing just the right touch of variety without destroying the essential unity of the tune. They add to our delight by returning in the final phrase as the sailor sings of his intention to return.

Here is a verse of a Scottish lament that might be set to music in a similar style:

Coronach

He is gone on the mountain,
    He is lost to the forest,
Like a summer-dried fountain,
    When our need was the sorest.
The font, reappearing,
    From the rain-drops shall borrow,
But to us comes no cheering,
    To Duncan no morrow!

                        Walter Scott

So far we have looked at Aeolian melodies. Let us now turn our attention to the Dorian mode. In 'Personent Hodie' we have a magnificent example of a Dorian tune. Sing it rhythmically and enjoy its rugged grandeur.

Here are some questions for you to consider.

How does this tune achieve unity and variety?

How do you account for its length (eighteen bars, as opposed to the more usual sixteen)?

How should it be phrased?

How should it be performed to make its best effect?

Here are more verses to set to music. Write in either the Aeolian or Dorian mode as seems the more appropriate. Experiment with different forms and do not be satisfied with first thoughts. Make a habit of revising and work carefully until each setting is as polished as you can make it. (The verses were taken from *Come Hither*, an anthology of poems chosen by Walter de la Mare and published by Constable.)

A Grace

Here a little child I stand
Heaving up my either hand,
Cold as paddocks though they be,
Here I lift them up to Thee,
For a benison to fall
On our meat and on us all.

Herrick

Cold Blows the Wind

Cauld blows the wind frae north to south,
  And drift is driving sairly;
The sheep are couring in the heugh,
  Oh sirs; it's winter fairly.
Now up in the morning's no' for me,
  Up in the morning early;
I'd rather gae supperless to my bed,
  Than rise in the morning early.

John Hamilton

The Bell-Man

From noise of Scare-fires rest ye free,
From murders—*Benedicite.*
From all mischances, that may fright
Your pleasing slumbers in the night:
Mercie secure ye all, and keep
The Goblin from ye, while ye sleep.
Past one aclock, and almost two,
My Masters all, *Good day to you!*

Herrick

HARMONY

In Book I you were introduced to the Primary and Secondary triads of the major scale (Ionian mode).

The same six chords are employed when harmonizing Aeolian and Dorian melodies.

In the Ionian mode the tonic and dominant chords are major. You will notice that in the Aeolian and Dorian modes the corresponding chords are minor.

As you would therefore expect, in the harmonization of Aeolian and Dorian melodies minor chords tend to predominate, particularly at the beginning and end of pieces and at some of the intermediate cadences. It is at these points that the distinctive modal flavour is most strongly felt.

Sing the following extract and accompany yourself at the piano. Then practise transposing the passage until you can perform it fluently a tone or a semitone higher or lower.

Quite often in modal tunes we come across phrases that are definitely Ionian in character and afford an opportunity for the introduction of a number of major triads with consequent contrast and variety. The 'B' phrase in 'High Germany' is a good example of this. Suppose we provide a piano accompaniment to this tune. Since it is a brisk and lively melody, we decide upon a sparse chordal accompaniment that will give sparkle to the rhythm without being too obtrusive.

We begin by jotting down the triads that are likely to provide the harmonic framework. At the same time we are thinking of the way in which they might be used to provide a rhythmic counterpoint to the tune. Our first sketch might appear as follows:

Once we are satisfied with the effectiveness of our harmonic outline the final accompaniment will soon take shape. In this case we have chosen simply to 'shadow' the tune.

High Germany

10

Practise improvising accompaniments to the tunes you have already met in this chapter together with those that follow. Provide written accompaniments to some of them, indicating appropriate tempi and dynamics.

1.

Here are two modal pieces for you to sing in harmony. 'Personent Hodie' you already know. We have chosen D as the final of the mode so that you may readily perceive its Dorian character, but we suggest that in performance you might prefer to transpose it up a tone or a minor third. Enjoy the minor chords in the opening phrase, and notice the strong effect of minor progressions whose roots are a fifth or a fourth apart. Notice, too, the touches of Ionian tonality that bring variety (e.g. bars 4–5 and 11–12).

Personent Hodie

(For further Latin words and for an English translation, see the *Oxford Book of Carols,* No. 78.)

'Matthew, Mark and Luke and John' is a beautiful folk-carol in the Phrygian mode. This mode has its own distinctive final cadence:

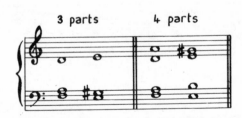

Have you heard this cadence in the music of Bach and Handel? Look through the score of Bach's third Brandenburg Concerto for a famous example.

Matthew, Mark and Luke and John

2 God is the branch and I the flower,
   Pray God send me a bless'd hour,
I go to bed some sleep to take,
   The Lord he knows if I shall wake,
Sleep I ever, wake I never,
   God receive my soul for ever.

Notice that this setting of 'Matthew, Mark and Luke and John' does not confine itself to the six triads that we have been discussing. Once you have acquired a feeling for modal tonality and can handle the basic progressions fluently you should experiment in your creative work with modern treatments of modal tunes. Here, for example, is Bartók's harmonization of a Hungarian melody in the Dorian mode:

Explore the music of Vaughan Williams, Holst, Ravel, Bartók, and Kodály. Study the following works and try to hear performances:

Vaughan Williams	*Fantasia on a theme of Thomas Tallis*
	English Folk-Songs Suite
	Mass in G minor
Holst	*Hymn of Jesus*
	St. Paul's Suite
Ravel	*Introduction and Allegro,* for harp, string quartet, flute and clarinet
	Piano Trio
Bartók	*Fifteen Hungarian Peasant Songs*
Kodály	*Psalmus Hungaricus*
	Missa Brevis

Take every opportunity of singing medieval and renaissance music. Learn by heart some of the famous plainsong melodies and find out as much as you can about the connection between plainsong and folk-song. Discuss your findings with your group. Here are two plainsong melodies that you should know:

Dies Irae

Pange Lingua

Consult the *English Hymnal* (No. 351) for the remaining stanzas of the *Dies Irae,* and notice the structural plan of the complete melody:

	A	A	B	B	C	C	A	A	B	B	C	C	A	A	B	B	C	D	E
Verse	1	2	3	4	5	6	7	8	9	10	11	12	13	14	15	16	17	18	19

This famous Gregorian sequence is described in the *Harvard Dictionary of Music* as being 'among the most impressive products of medieval poetry and music', and a number of composers have introduced its foreboding phrases into their compositions. Listen to the last movement of the *Symphonie fantastique* by Berlioz for a fine example.

CHAPTER TWO

THE MINOR SCALE

The Harmonic Minor Scale

Sing and play these quotations.

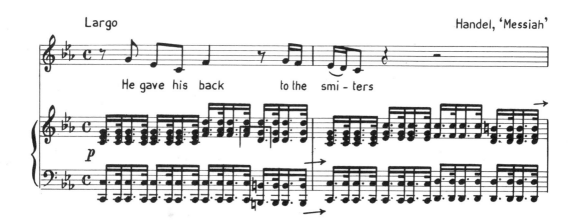

He gave his back   to the smi – ters

Ⅴ

Purcell and Handel have used repeated notes, suspensions, and violent, jerky rhythms in these powerful emotional outbursts. The minor intervals (e.g. at ⌐‾‾‾¬) are, however, equally vital factors in the pathos so strikingly expressed.

J. S. Bach

(Fugue subject from 'The 48' Book I)

In this example from Bach, notice particularly the contrast between the major seventh (B♮) on the one hand, and the minor sixth (A♭) and minor third (E♭) on the other. To make yourself more vividly aware of this major/minor conflict, play the fugue subject a few times as though written in C major, with the third, sixth, and seventh all major; then return to the correct version.

Let us now compare the Harmonic Minor Scale, first with the Major Scale (Ionian Mode), and then with the Aeolian Mode.

Major scale   Harmonic Minor scale

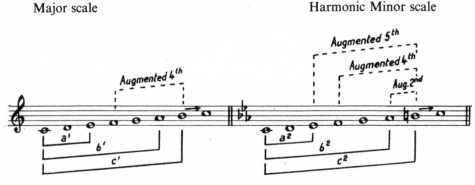

The major scale has its third and sixth degrees major, whereas in the harmonic minor scale these are minor.

Both scales have the upward-leaning major seventh (Leading Note).

The harmonic minor scale includes the somewhat strained, angular intervals of the augmented second, fourth, and fifth, whereas the major scale has only one augmented interval, the fourth.

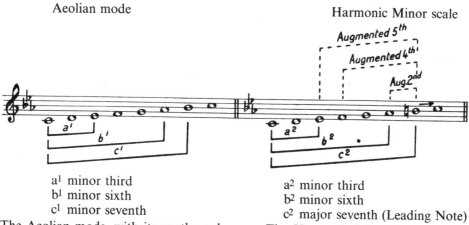

Aeolian mode   Harmonic Minor scale

a¹ minor third — a² minor third

a^1 minor third
b^1 minor sixth
c^1 minor seventh

a^2 minor third
b^2 minor sixth
c^2 major seventh (Leading Note)

The Aeolian mode, with its gentle, only mildly dissonant minor seventh, has quiet dignity and spiritual beauty.

The Harmonic Minor scale is restless and dramatic in its sharp clashes of the major seventh, augmented second and augmented fourth.

Augmented intervals are not very commonly found in melody; they are often felt to be harsh and to militate against a flowing style. In Book I we demonstrated the tendency of the augmented fourth to resolve outwards.

Nevertheless, there is no 'rule' (except in elementary examinations) against using the augmented fourth melodically. It is in fact to be found in a variety of beautiful themes:

20

hangs — where shelled roads part. _____ In this

war _____ He too lost a limb.

© 1962 by Boosey & Hawkes Music Publishers Ltd.

Augmented intervals are, however, often found in passages involving
sequences. (SEQUENCE: a melodic pattern repeated at a different pitch.)

J.S. Bach, 'St. Matthew Passion'

The technical means by which Bach here expresses searing grief are inter-dependent. They include a particular choice of instrumental colour, a characteristic rhythmic figure repeated many times and a throbbing bass.

Let us particularly notice, however,

(a) the augmented seconds and augmented fourths in the melody
(b) the minor seconds in the melody
(c) the compound minor seconds (minor ninths) in the harmony.

At the beginning of bar 1 we have V7 in the key of B minor:

In the middle of the bar, V7 has become a dominant ninth:

The V9 resolves, not on to the chord of B minor, but on to that of B major. This latter now serves as V in the key of E minor.

As we play the L.H. part of this piano transcription, we notice that the augmented second has been avoided by the sharpening of the sixth degree.

Instead of: we have:

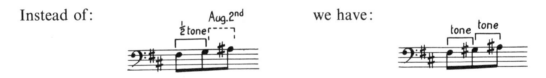

This observation leads us to a consideration of the Melodic Minor scale.

The Melodic Minor Scale

The pungent tension of the augmented second is avoided in the melodic minor scale.

---

* Small letters are used to indicate the minor mode.

Note that the descending form differs from the ascending. The descending form corresponds to the Aeolian mode. In the ascending form, both sixth and seventh degrees are sharpened. The major sixth leads smoothly to the major seventh. Contrast with the harmonic minor scale.

Great care is needed in deciding whether the harmonic or melodic minor scale is the more appropriate in any particular passage. Play these quotations from Bach's French Suite No. 2 in C minor:

Bar 1 The R.H. plays part of the ascending melodic minor scale, giving a pleasantly fluent lead-up to the lovely minor third at the top of the phrase. This is followed by an Interrupted Cadence, V–VI, in which the minor sixth (harmonic minor scale) is essential in the bass.

Bar 2 The minor sixth is now used expressively at the top of the phrase in the R.H., and the leading note appears in the L.H. (harmonic minor scale). The second R.H. phrase begins as though in sequence with the corresponding phrase in the previous bar, but this time the rhythmic figure is developed. At the end of the quotation the minor seventh in the L.H. leads down to the minor sixth (melodic minor).

Bar 3 The minor seventh in the L.H. leads down to the syncopated minor sixth (melodic minor).

Bar 4 The major seventh (leading note) is used in the Imperfect cadence.

Describe to your Tutor how the harmonic and melodic scales have been used in the Air and Menuet.

Melody

Sing and play responsive phrases to the following openings:

Harmony

Compare the effect of cadences in the major and minor systems. Sing all these examples carefully. Play them in other keys.

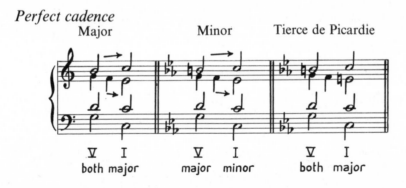

When a composition in the minor mode ends with a major chord the third in this chord is known as the 'Tierce de Picardie'. For centuries after the emergence of major/minor tonality composers tended to relieve the 'sadness' and dissonance of the minor mode by ending with a major chord or by omitting the third in the final chord (see Mozart's 'Requiem').

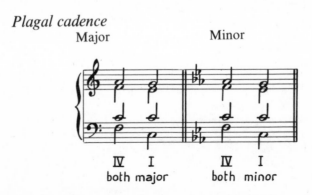

Interrupted cadence

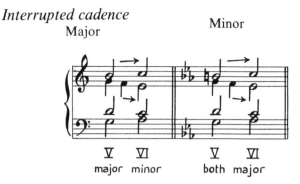

Note particularly the striking effect of the Interrupted cadence in the minor mode. The bass rises a semitone and chord VI is a major chord. The major third is usually doubled and this adds to the brightness and 'surprise'.

Imperfect cadence
The final chord is always V with a major third.
    Play these examples first in C major and then in C minor.
    Analyse the chords in each cadence.

Harmonizing the Melodic Minor Scale

N.B.
  (a) III is a useful major chord to harmonize the descending minor seventh.
  (b) II here is a diminished triad and considered by some authorities to be weak when used in the root position. It is usual to have it in first inversion (IIb) or to add the seventh (II7, II7b, II7c or II7d).
  (c) II here is a minor triad and is therefore used freely in root position or first inversion.
  (d) V7c is known as the 'Rising Seventh'; it is equally effective to allow the seventh to rise or to fall. (In all other positions of V7 the seventh normally falls.)
  (e) Unequal fifths (diminished fifth—perfect fifth, or vice versa), are commonly used consecutively, provided that the lowest moving part in the harmony is not involved.

26

Harmonize these tunes at the piano:

Chrisimus Day

Patapan

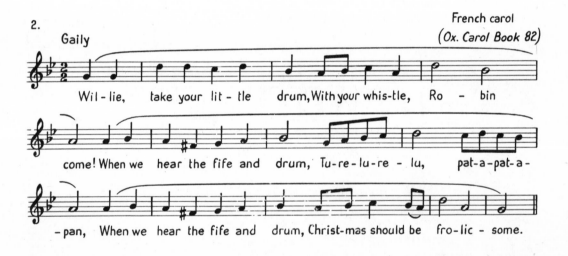

The Old Man from Lee

French Carol from Provence

(used by Bizet in 'L'Arlésienne')

4.
Alla marcia

Write simple arrangements for violin and piano of these two fragments from Schumann's *Album for the Young*, Op. 68.

5.
Lamentoso

'Popular Song'

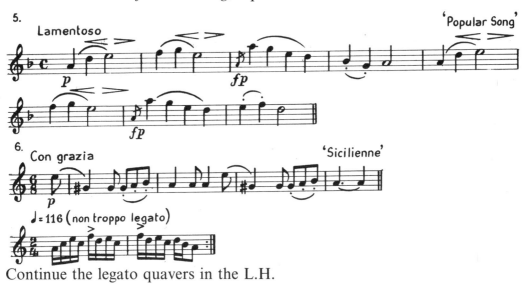

6.
Con grazia

'Sicilienne'

♩=116 (non troppo legato)

Continue the legato quavers in the L.H.

7.
Allegro ma non troppo

Domenico Scarlatti, Sonata in B minor

legato

Complete the cello part of bars 1–4 and the violin part of bars 5–8 in the following extract from the slow movement of the 'Italian' Symphony.

8.

Add a L.H. part in accordance with the rhythm indicated. Use octaves in bars 1–8, and two parts in bars 9–16.

9.

CHAPTER THREE

MODULATION

The Relative Major and the Relative Minor

In considering the folk-song 'High Germany' in Chapter I, we noticed that although the first and last phrases are Aeolian, the second and third phrases each end in the Ionian mode.

Our next example shows a change from the minor to the major mode. Sing the song and experiment with the harmonies at the piano.

David of the White Rock

Poco lento e molto espressivo

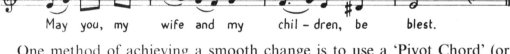

Bring me, said Da – vid, my harp yet a – gain;

Ere death can take me, I'd play one last strain.

Un – til I've touched those dear strings, I'll not rest.

May you, my wife and my chil – dren, be blest.

One method of achieving a smooth change is to use a 'Pivot Chord' (or 'stepping-stone'), i.e. a chord that is common to both keys.

e: I
G: VI   Ib IIb V⁷c   I

The chord of E minor is Tonic (I) in the key of E minor and Submediant (VI) in that of G major.

In returning from G major to E minor, our pivot chord might be A minor:

Ib G: II
    e: IV IIb V⁷d Ib

Notice in bars 1 and 2, the note E repeated from a weak beat to a strong beat. Emphasis may be obtained by treating it as a suspension or as a seventh. Compare these possibilities:

(a) The F♯ is an accented passing note; the repeated E is a seventh.
(b) The F♯ is a harmony note; the E is a suspension.
(c) The F♯ is a harmony note; the E–D♯ is harmonized with a cadential $^6_4$ (feminine ending).

Devise your own accompaniment to 'David of the White Rock', making sure that the piano part flows on from one phrase to the next, e.g.

Comment upon the tonality in this quotation:

Here are two examples for you to sing in class.

Complete the chord indications. Notice Purcell's use of the diminished triad in root position. What is the effect of a high proportion of chords in root position?

Rehearse carefully the pianissimo entries and learn to sustain the long phrases of the beautiful quotation from *Gerontius* on the next page before considering the following observations regarding the harmony:

(a) Elgar uses the calm and gentle IIIb–V–I in the final cadence, rather than the more obvious Ic–V–I, or the strong V13–I.

(b) When a note is repeated or held over from a weaker to a stronger position in the bar, it usually becomes a suspension or the seventh of a chord, e.g.

Bars 4–5 F in the bass becomes the seventh of V7d in C minor and resolves on the second beat of the bar.

Bar 5 Eb in the bass becomes a suspension on the third beat of the bar and resolves on the fourth beat.

Bars 5–6 Ab in the soprano becomes a suspension on the first beat of bar 6.

Indicate to your Tutor other suspensions in this quotation.

(c) Compare the first three beats of bars 3 and 5—

The rhythm of the soprano is identical.

The melody progresses from the fifth to the sixth degrees of the scale (E♭ major in bar 3, C minor in bar 5).

The harmonic progression V7d–Ib is found in each case. Thus we have a Modulating Sequence.

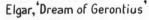
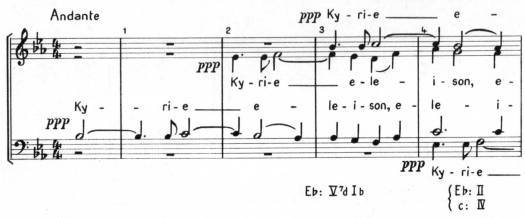

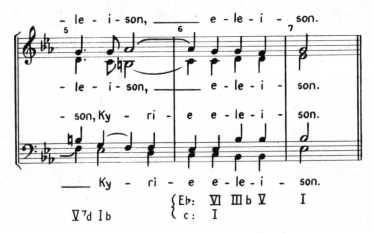

Modulating Sequences

Each phrase of a modulating sequence must include a progression which clearly and unmistakably defines the key. The leading note moves to the tonic in each of the following progressions:

C: I V⁷c Ib a: I V⁷c Ib C: I VIIb Ib a: I VIIb Ib

(a) and (b) the forms of inverted perfect cadence most often found in modulating sequences.

(c), (d), and (e) three progressions that differ only slightly:

    (c) the 'Passing $^6_4$', the bass moves in contrary motion with another part;

    (d) the 'Rising Seventh', the inversion of V7 in which the seventh may rise *or* fall;

    (e) VIIb, first inversion of a diminished triad—musically rather more pleasing than either the passing $^6_4$ or the rising seventh.

(A reminder: 'unequal fifths', i.e. a perfect fifth followed by a diminished fifth, or a diminished fifth followed by a perfect fifth, are effective, provided the lowest moving part in the harmony is not involved).

Modulating sequences normally include some form of inverted perfect or interrupted cadence. Each phrase of the sequence includes two chords that establish the key. Sing and play this simple progression beginning in C major, modulating by means of a sequence to the relative minor, and returning via a pivot chord to the tonic.

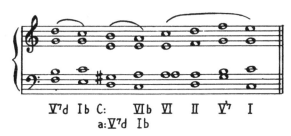

V⁷d Ib C: VIb VI II V⁷ I
a:V⁷d Ib

Add suspensions:

Single (a), double (b), and triple (c) suspensions are effective in the upper parts, provided the bass sings a harmony note. At (c) the leading note falls to complete the chord.

Single suspensions only, however, are usual when the bass has the note that causes the dissonance (d).

Let each student improvise a melody while the class sustains the harmonies, e.g.

Let the girls sustain the upper notes of the harmony while the men improvise a bass part, e.g.

Experiment at the piano. Play the five examples above with pianistic realizations of the given harmonic progression.

Suppose we now incorporate our modulating sequence into a musical structure of sixteen bars, beginning in A minor, modulating to the relative major and then returning to the tonic.

Write a group of contrasted dances for piano based on this harmonic framework. Here are three suggested openings:

Devise other harmonic progressions and transpose them into all keys, e.g.

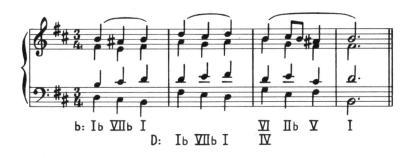

Tunes to harmonize at the piano

Setting chorus parts for SAB

(Instrumental introductions according to the resources of the members of a group, piano accompaniments, and chorus parts.)

Consider this folk-song—you will find four other verses in the *Penguin Book of English Folk-Songs*.

The Gentleman Soldier

We decide to treat the verse as 'happy-go-lucky' and flexible, but the chorus, with its onomatopoeic, drum-and-fife references, as martial and aggressive. $\frac{6}{8}$ changes from gentle rocking to vigorous marching.

As a motif for the Introduction we chose the 'rap-a-tap tap' rhythm and devise raucous instrumentation.

We prefer the bright key of A major. The sopranos are happier with their lowest note as C♯, while the increased range released for the altos gives us more scope to manoeuvre an enjoyable middle line.

things can ne – ver be, _____ for mar-ried I am al – rea-dy, _____ and

chil – dren I have three. _____ Two wives are al-lowed in the

ar _____ my, but one's too ma – ny for me!' _____

CHORUS

For the drums did go with a rap-a-tap tap and the fifes did loud-ly play, _ Say-ing,

For the drums did go with a rap-a-tap tap, the fifes did loud-ly play, _

For the drums did go with a rap-a-tap tap and a rap-a-ta, tap-a-ta tap, _ Say-ing,

This song might easily have been harmonized entirely in the major mode, but we prefer to make brief excursions to the relative minor. In bar 2 of the chorus, the introduction of the new leading note and the contrary motion semitones between the alto and bass give a sharp edge to the 'rap-a-tap tap'. (The D is an accented auxiliary note). The effect in bar 6 is less striking and hardly worthy of the description 'modulation'. We might prefer to think of the E♯ as a chromatic auxiliary note.

Notice the contrast between the vocal and instrumental styles. How easy the arrangement is to perform, yet how difficult it would be to sing the piano part and play the voice parts! Jumping about in 8ves and sixths is as simple on the piano as insistently repeating notes is in singing.

In the Introduction, the blustery piccolo and side-drum are matched by percussive dissonances in the piano, but in the accompaniment of the verse the piano is used more melodically.

The repeated 'rap-a-tap's and the insistent quavers in the bass of the chorus encourage a realistic imitation of the side-drum. The altos, however, are allowed a brief opportunity to catch both the percussive 'rap-a-tap' of the drums and also the melodic 'play' of the fifes. By omitting two unessential words and in the last phrase adjusting the emphasis, we are able to include three quaver rests. These tiny silences in one part help to avoid congestion in the scoring.

Here are two songs for you to set for solo, chorus and piano. Some emphasis on the third degree of the scale is needed, and this may be obtained by using V13 or by modulating to the relative minor.

1. Merrily *The Lincolnshire Poacher*

The Tree in the Bog

Here is a possible treatment for the last bar leading back to the first bar:

† Sharpening the fifth is a freakish device, effective here in helping to drive forward the rhythm in a song that has many verses.

* Chromatic passing notes

In the remaining songs to set for solo, chorus, and piano, we leave you to decide whether modulation is necessary or desirable.

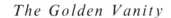

The Golden Vanity

Notice the effective use of the first inversion of an augmented triad (IIIb in the minor mode).

Death and the Lady

'Shadow' the melody in an unobtrusive way, and do nothing that will tend to impede the flexibility of the phrasing. Set the final phrase for two, three, or four voices.

Down Among the Dead Men

Complete the missing harmonies of the following quotations, carefully maintaining the style of the given parts. Afterwards, compare your version with the original.

CHAPTER FOUR

MODULATION TO THE DOMINANT

Here are three arrangements of a well-known nursery song.

Points to note:
(1) Harmonic rhythm:

The harmonies are simple and diatonic, and disjunct movement in the added part makes for humour and an instrumental style.
(2) The harmonic rhythm is more eventful:

Conjunct movement in the added parts makes for a lyrical, cantabile effect. The transitory glimpse of C major in bar 2 adds a touch of colour without upsetting the prevailing tonality of F major.

(3) Our nursery song has now assumed the dignity of a chorale. Harmonic rhythm:

Because of the slower tempo, the excursion into C major now makes a more pronounced effect: the time-factor has altered the situation.

At the two cadence bars (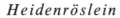), the harmonies correspond, and the bass moves disjunctly. This gives weight and balance to the harmony, and draws attention to the tune's two-part structure.

Here is a variation of our nursery song for you to sing in harmony. Notice particularly the effect of the five-bar phrase that arises from the repetition of bar 2. Try the effect of omitting bar 3 in performance. You will agree that the interpolation brings charm and freshness to the music.

Let us now listen to Schubert making the same journey, from F to C and home again, but over a longer time span.

Heidenröslein

46

Notice that the tonic key is firmly established in the first four bars. Then comes the modulating phrase (bars 5–10), with the F major chord as a pivot. Observe how skilfully Schubert employs the dominant seventh to establish the new tonality. He introduces it three times in this second phrase. First it appears in its last inversion, resolving on to Ib. Next, it appears in root position, to be followed by VI (interrupted, or 'deceptive' cadence). Only at the end of the phrase is V7 followed by I in root position. Suppose that this progression had been used in bar 8. The curve of the phrase would then have been broken and the music halted prematurely. As it is, the music flows smoothly forward and the perfect cadence is all the more effective when it eventually arrives.

After the modulation the music returns immediately to the tonic key, and this is clearly re-established by the use of dominant and tonic harmony. Finally, the piano rounds off the song with a brief, poetic postlude. (Note that in performance this postlude might well be used as an introduction. It would serve to set the mood, tempo and pitch, and would be an altogether more musical procedure than striking a chord, however discreetly). The song as a whole is sixteen bars long, but we notice that it does not divide into the familiar pattern of four equal phrases, but into 4+6+4+2. And, as in the Czech carol, it is the modulating phrase that is extended. In both cases we realize that the composer wishes us to share his delight as he savours the change of tonality.

Here are some verses for you to set to music, using a similar design to that employed by Schubert in 'Heidenröslein'.

Tonic	How many miles to Babylon?
	Threescore and ten, Sir.
Dominant	Can I get there by candlelight?
	Oh yes, and back again, Sir.
(Extension)	Oh yes, and back again.
Tonic	If your heels are nimble and light,
	You may get there by candlelight.
Postlude	

Begin as follows:

Make sure of your bearings before you begin by noting the four triads that are common to E♭ and its dominant, B♭.

Remember the leading note in the dominant key—A♮. Avoid A♭'s and A♮'s in juxtaposition as you make your modulation. Pivot smoothly by ensuring that the common triads form a satisfactory progression, e.g.

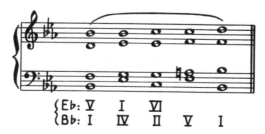

48

Here is a selection of tunes which modulate to the dominant and then return directly to the tonic key. Practise harmonizing them at the keyboard until you can modulate fluently.

Make an arrangement for soloist, chorus (SAB), and piano of this Northumbrian shanty. Provide parts for the members of your group to rehearse.

Billy Boy

2 Is she fit to be your wife?
She's as fit to be me wife
As the fork is to the knife.

3 Can she cook a bit o' steak?
She can cook a bit o' steak,
Aye, and make a girdle cake.

4 Can she make an Irish stew?
She can make an Irish stew,
Aye, and 'Singing Hinnies' too.

Arrange this German folk-song for unaccompanied voices (SATB). Write smooth, grateful parts, and aim at a truly vocal effect, taking particular care over phrasing and dynamics.

Die Lorelei

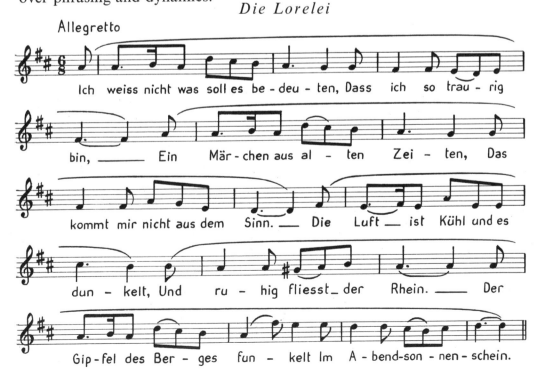

50

2 Die schönste Jungfrau sitzet
  Dort oben wunderbar,
Ihr goldenes Geshmeide blitzet,
  Sie kämmt sich ihr goldenes Haar.
  Sie kämmt es mit goldenem Kamme
  Und singt ein Lied dabei,
Das hat eine wundersame
  Gewaltige Melodei.

3 Den Schiffer im kleinen Schiffe
  Ergreift es mit wilden Weh;
Er sieht nicht die Felsenriffe,
  Er schaut nur hinauf in die Höh.
Ich glaube, die Wellen verschlingen
  Am Ende noch Schiffer und Kahn;
Und das hat mit ihrem Singen
  Die Lorelei gethan.

You have practised modulating from tonic to dominant in major tonality, and we now turn our attention to the corresponding modulation in minor tonality. This modulation occurs much less frequently than its major counterpart as the tonal design for a short composition. If you examine a representative selection of short pieces in the minor mode, you will find that composers tend to modulate to the relative major or the submediant major rather than to the dominant minor. This is partly explained by the fact that a minor key and its dominant minor have only one chord in common (if we take the distinctive harmonic minor mode as a basis for comparison).

As you will see, the C minor chord (I in the tonic key, IV in the dominant), is the only triad common to both keys. Here are Schumann and Bach using the tonic chord as a pivot:

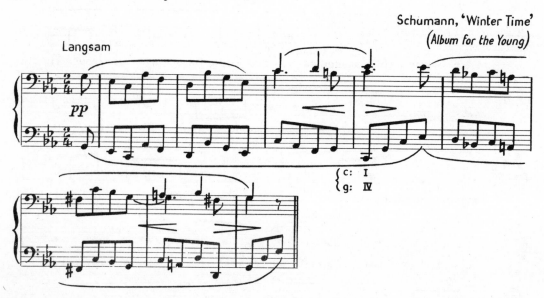

Schumann, 'Winter Time'
(Album for the Young)

Play and sing responses to the following phrases. Let each of your phrases modulate to the dominant minor, and end in such a way as to imply a perfect or plagal cadence. Afterwards, write out your melodies and add a bass part to each. Think in terms of a duo for two particular instruments (e.g. violin and cello, or clarinet and bassoon), and phrase accordingly. Make sure that your bass parts are flowing and melodious and that they are rhythmically independent of the tunes they partner.

Complete the bass part in this quotation from Handel. In the original there is continuous quaver movement until the final note, which is a crotchet.

Complete the following extract, preserving the style of the opening bars, i.e. the L.H. has octaves throughout in the rhythm indicated and the R.H. has two- or three-note chords.

Harmonize the two following passages for SATB. Purcell gives all four voices the same rhythm except in the penultimate bar where the alto has a touch of independence.

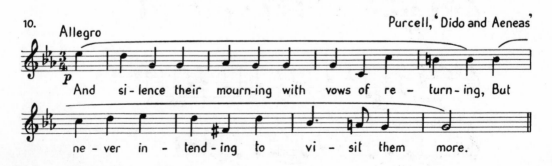

In the next chapter we shall continue to investigate modulation. As we venture further afield and discover new resources you will be able to extend the range of your compositions. We shall begin to invent short movements in the style of those found in the classical suite and so, by way of preparation for this, we now introduce the FIGURED BASS.

This is fundamental to Baroque music in which there was an element of improvisation. Looking at the score of a flute sonata by Handel, we see that only the solo part and a figured bass are written. The keyboard player was expected to improvise a suitable accompaniment based on the harmonies implied by the figures. This called for considerable musicianship of the kind that we hope you are developing.

Let us examine a passage from a Handel sonata and see how the system operates.

The figures imply that the following harmonies are to be used:

Here are some of the signs with which you should be acquainted:

Sign	Meaning	Example
(1) No sign	Root position chord	
(2) 6 (short for $\frac{6}{3}$)	First inversion	
(3) $\frac{6}{4}$	Second inversion	
(4) 7 (short for $\frac{7}{5}{3}$)	Seventh chord in root position	
(5) $\frac{6}{5}$ (short for $\frac{6}{5}{3}$)	Seventh chord, first inversion	
(6) $\frac{4}{3}$ (short for $\frac{6}{4}{3}$)	Seventh chord, second inversion	
(7) $\frac{4}{2}$ (short for $\frac{6}{4}{2}$)	Seventh chord, third inversion	
(8) ♯, ♭ or ♮	Applies to the third of the chord	
(9) ♯, ♭ or ♮ before or after a figure, e.g. ♮7	Applies to the seventh from the bass (or its compound interval)	
(10) ——	Passing, auxiliary or subsidiary harmony notes present in the bass; upper parts to remain unchanged for the duration of the dash	
(11) ⑥, ⑦	Different usages with different composers; usually implies the presence of the diminished triad	
(12) 98, 76, 43	Suspensions or appoggiaturas	

The art of playing from figured bass is a study in itself and we can do no more than hint at it here. We hope you will explore the standard works on the subject. Take every opportunity of listening to authentic performances of Baroque music and notice how the continuo part is played by eminent musicians. Remember that the figures are a guide; they leave room for individuality in performance.

Here are five realizations of the Handel bass. Play them over and discuss their style and suitability with members of your group.

Before we leave the Handel quotation there is a further point we should consider, namely the harmonies at the cadence. As major and minor tonality displaced the ecclesiastical modes, certain modal turns of phrase still lingered on, and the passage under discussion shows the influence of the Phrygian mode. Compare the following:

The progression used by Handel occurs frequently in music from Baroque times onward and you should be familiar with it. Practise transposing the following version until you can reproduce it fluently at any pitch.

Here is a Larghetto movement from a Handel sonata for recorder and continuo. Practise playing from the figured bass. Then rehearse the movement with a recorder player and give a performance to your friends.

Larghetto · Handel, Recorder sonata

It seems fitting that we should close this chapter with a quotation from a masterpiece of Baroque music. We have chosen a passage from Purcell's *Dido and Aeneas* for you to sing. It comes from the final pages of the opera and is sung by the chorus after the death of Dido.

The key is G minor. Notice the modulation to the dominant minor and the perfect cadence in bars 8–9. The music then returns to the tonic key and passes through the relative major in bars 10–12 before closing in G minor. Notice too, the expressive part-writing and the beautiful nuances and rhythmic effects. The opening phrase, 'Soft and gentle as her heart' is set in polyphonic style with imitative entries and independent movement. The answering strain, 'Keep here your watch, and never part,' is more homophonic. Reflect on the dramatic and expressive effect of the rests, and particularly in the final phrases as the chorus sing the word 'never'. Rehearse the passage carefully and pay special attention to intonation and phrasing.

Study Edward J. Dent's imaginative realization of Purcell's bass in the vocal score published by OUP.

Why not consider a stage production? The opera was written for Josias Priest's school for girls in Chelsea, and was first performed there about 1689. You will find it most rewarding in performance.

CHAPTER FIVE
MODULATION TO CLOSELY-RELATED KEYS

Here is a Handel minuet for you to play. Begin by playing melody and bass only, and notice how effective these two parts are in themselves.

Now play an arrangement in three-part harmony. Let the R.H. provide the inner part for most of the time. It should not be elaborate; let it move mainly in crotchets and minims. Think in terms of an instrumental trio; this will help to ensure that your part has character and is not merely 'filling-in'.

Next, experiment with the introduction of occasional four-part harmonies, but be careful not to overload the texture. Let the total effect be one of lightness and clarity, and remember that thicker sonorities are more telling when used sparingly.

Notice the absence of phrase marks and dynamics. Handel has avoided precise indications of how the piece is to be performed and has left us free to exercise our musical insight and initiative in deciding upon a suitable interpretation.

Before we examine the structure of the minuet, there are certain preliminaries concerning tonality about which you should be clear. In Western music, as you know, we divide the octave into twelve semitones and build our scales in a cycle of perfect fifths. The clock face, therefore, with its twelve divisions is a very useful symbol. It enables us to demonstrate the cycle of tonality pictorially, and at the same time our attention is drawn to the degree of relationship that exists between the various keys of the cycle.

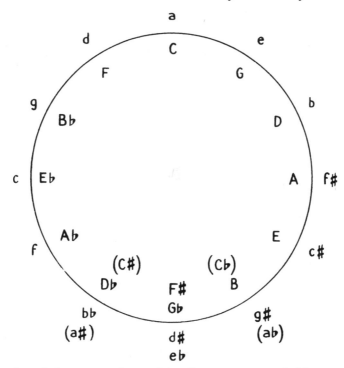

All keys are related, but a tonic and its five nearest neighbours in the tonal cycle are said to be *closely* related. Thus, for example, if we select F major as a tonic, we see that its five nearest neighbours are—

d (relative minor)
C (dominant)
a (relative minor of the dominant)
B♭ (subdominant)
g (relative minor of the subdominant)

In general terms, the relationships are as follows:

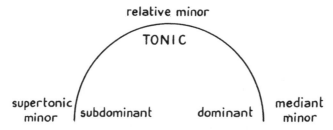

Let us now return to our consideration of the Handel minuet. Here is the structure:

62

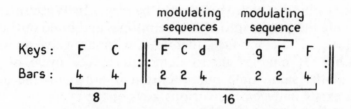

The minuet is in two parts, each of which is to be played twice. This binary form is one of the basic structures of Baroque music and you will find it employed in a wide variety of pieces ranging from simple, non-modulating movements to long, highly-organized masterpieces. One particular structure figured prominently towards the end of the period, and since modulation is such an integral part of musical form we shall discuss this design in some detail.

Binary Form as commonly found in Baroque Movements

In a movement in the major mode, modulation in the first part is usually to the dominant or relative minor. Minor movements tend to modulate to the relative major or dominant minor. Other keys may be touched upon in the course of the first section, depending on its length and the nature of the music. In a short piece there may be no modulation in the first part, and in such cases we frequently find the first section ending with an imperfect cadence in the tonic key.

The second part normally begins in the key established at the end of part one with some reference to the thematic material of the opening bars. The second part tends to be longer than the first and to contain more modulation. This is the place where we might expect to find modulating sequences. The amount of modulation varies, but such as there is remains within the orbit of the five closely-related keys.

Very often the melodic phrases and harmonic progressions used in the closing bars of the first part (in a related key) will be used again in the closing bars of the movement (in the tonic key), thus giving balance and symmetry to the total design. These phrases and progressions may also appear at important intermediate cadences.

With these observations in mind, let us return to the Handel minuet to note the following points:

Part One modulates to the dominant.

Part Two does not begin in this key. There is a brief return to the tonic and the music passes through C major for the second time on its way to D minor. Thematically, the two parts are related: both begin with the interval of a fourth. This interval figures prominently in the modulating sequences at the beginning of Part Two (bars 9–14).

After the opening eight bars, which are serene and flowing, the modulating sequences, with their rising movement and short, two-bar phrases, bring a feeling of 'urgency' and development to the music. In the next sequence (bars 17–20), the interval of a fourth is expanded to that of a sixth. This wider leap gives added impetus and prepares for the climax in bar 21.

The same turns of phrase and harmonic progressions are used at the close of each section, and also at the cadence in D minor (bars 14–16).

Part One is eight bars long, as compared with sixteen bars in Part Two, and Part One contains one modulation (to C), whereas there are three modulations in Part Two (to C, D minor, and G minor).

Here, in outline, are six baroque movements of the type we have just described. Complete them by adding the requisite number of parts along the lines indicated.

In each case, begin by making sure that you are thoroughly familiar with the tonic and its five closely-related keys. Devise a short chordal progression (e.g. I–V–VI–Ib–IIb–V–I), and be able to play it fluently in all six keys.

When you have completed your settings consult the originals and discuss with your Tutor.

This Larghetto is in three-part harmony throughout. Complete by continuing the inner part in the style of the opening bars. Notice that it is for Violin III and Viola and consider how this will affect the range of the part you provide.

1.

64

Add a bass part for the next two examples. We have indicated the harmonic rhythm and the rhythm of the original bass. Modulating sequences are indicated thus:

Arrange the following Minuet for violin, viola, and cello.

4. Minuet   Handel, 'Berenice'

Complete the oboe parts in this Minuet and Trio by Telemann, maintaining the style of the opening bars. In the Trio the two oboes play together in harmony throughout and have this rhythm:

Realize the continuo part and devise some unobtrusive figuration when the oboes have long notes.

5.

Menuet   Telemann, Tafelmusik

Oboes

Continuo

66

Menuet da capo al 𝄐

The following Badinage and Trio are also from Telemann's *Tafelmusik*. Complete the oboe part in the Badinage and realize a part for harpsichord. Study the rhythms and phrase-lengths of the oboe's opening bars and maintain the same style in your added part. Then complete the cello part in the Trio. Telemann makes a feature of repeated notes and gives the cello an unbroken flow of quavers until the final note, which is a minim.

The harmonic rhythm from * is as follows:

pedal note

pedal note

Da capo al 𝄐

6. Badinage

Très vite

Telemann, Tafelmusik

Badinage da capo al 𝄐

Practise improvising responses to the following openings. Invent five different responses in each case, modulating in turn to each of the five closely-related keys. Make sure that your phrases are shapely and balanced and continue the ideas contained in the opening statement.

Examine as many scores as you can of suites, partitas, ordres, lessons, sonatas, and concertos, by Bach, Handel, Corelli, Scarlatti, Vivaldi, Purcell, Rameau, and Couperin, and study the way in which these composers have employed binary form. Select certain movements for careful analysis, paying special attention to their tonal schemes.

You should then go on to compose a short suite in baroque style. You need not necessarily think in terms of the keyboard, but whatever medium you adopt, let the various movements be in the same key. Confine your modulations to the five closely-related keys but do not follow the same modulatory scheme in each piece.

70

Secondary Dominants

So far in our discussion of modulation we have not attempted to define the term precisely, believing that it would be confusing to make too many distinctions in the early stages of study. All excursions into new tonality have been accepted as modulations, however brief they may have been.

But if modulation is taken to mean the establishment of a new tonal centre in such a way that the original tonic is definitely displaced, then clearly a brief glance of new tonality in a phrase which is predominantly diatonic cannot fairly be described as a modulation. For example, in the following passage by Schubert, the music does not modulate to D minor and A minor at (a) and (b): the phrase is firmly rooted in C major.

Nor would it be correct to describe the touches of tonal colour at (a) and (b) as 'transitions' since the music is not passing from one key to another. Walter Piston in his treatise on harmony has pointed out that 'Any degree of the scale may be preceded by its own dominant without weakening the fundamental tonality,' and he has coined the term 'secondary dominant' in this connection. This is a valuable addition to musical terminology since it throws light on many passages that are not susceptible to explanation in terms of 'modulation' or 'transition'.

Consider the following extract from Mozart:

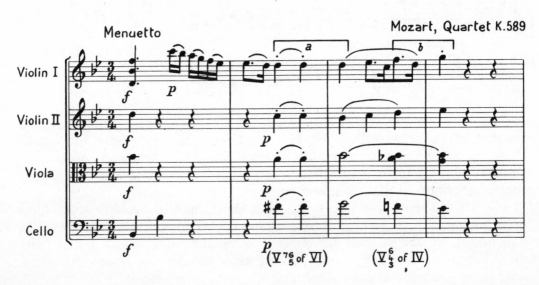

Above is a passage in B♭ major. At (a) and (b) chords VI and IV are preceded by their dominants and these secondary dominants bring colour to the music without undermining the prevailing tonality. The diminished seventh at * (a chord to be discussed in the next chapter) acts as an alternative to the secondary dominant of chord VI.

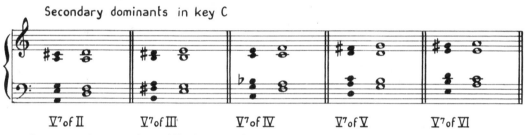

Invent phrases in differing styles, introducing each of these secondary dominants in turn, e.g.

Consult scores by Mozart, Beethoven, and Schubert and find examples of secondary dominants in non-modulating phrases.

CHAPTER SIX

CHROMATIC HARMONY

In previous chapters we have been concerned with diatonic harmony. Accidentals have appeared only

    (a) to sharpen, or to cancel the sharpening of, the sixth and seventh degrees in the minor mode,

    (b) in modulation, and in secondary dominants,

    (c) in unessential notes, e.g. chromatic passing and auxiliary notes and chromatic appoggiaturas.

Chromatic harmony involves chords containing one or more essential notes that are foreign to the scale of the key.

In most music of the 18th and early 19th centuries chromatic harmony is used sparingly and to achieve particularly colourful, expressive, or dramatic effect.

The chromatically altered notes of the Diminished Seventh chord in this quotation lean towards the root and fifth of the dominant chord and the tonality of G major is actually strengthened. Chord I6, the more obvious diatonic harmonization of the high G, acquires a special beauty as a relief from the chromatic chord, and one feels that a perfect balance between diatonic and chromatic harmony has been achieved.

In this chorale from Bach's Christmas Oratorio we again find ♯IV7, the diminished seventh chord built upon the raised subdominant.

Rehearse the chorale and work towards a convincing performance. Analyse the harmonies in detail. Notice the vivid interpretation of the words of the first line obtained through the dramatic modulation to the dominant. Contrast this strong effect with the tender expression of 'This Child now weak in infancy'. In the magnificent crescendo that follows, notice particularly the rising semitones in the bass.

The supertonic chromatic seventh,* II7♯3, with its major third, perfect fifth and minor seventh, is utterly different in effect from ♯IV7, with its minor third, diminished fifth and diminished seventh. II7♯3 in bar 10, has the intervals and vitality of a V7. (cf. Secondary Dominants, Chapter V).

Our next example introduces two more chromatic chords. Play this famous Prelude in C minor and then sing the vocal arrangement.

Chopin, Op. 28, N° 20

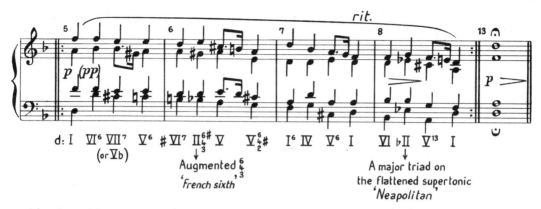

This simplified arrangement lacks the sonority and grandeur of the original but shows clearly

(a) the effective preparation and resolution of sevenths, arising as suspensions in the alto part in bars 1, 3–4, 5, and 5–6,

(b) that in the modulating sequence the seventh is added to chord IV only in the first phrase; in the major key IV7 is a major seventh and Chopin evidently preferred to avoid this pungent dissonance here,

(c) III6–I and V13–I in major and minor modes,

(d) that, in bars 5 and 6, minor intervals predominate in the bass, with its descending chromatic scale, and in the alto, with the tender motif characterized by the suspensions (prepared sevenths),

(e) an augmented sixth chord built upon the minor submediant and resolving on to dominant harmony in bar 6,

(f) that the major chord on the flattened supertonic in bar 8 (♭II or 'Neapolitan') is stern and arresting.

We now consider in detail the chromatic chords introduced.

The Diminished Seventh

In a previous chapter we met the diminished seventh in diatonic harmony. It is so found in the minor mode as chord VII7, which some authorities refer to as the 'dominant minor ninth without the root'.

Compare the effect of V, V7, V9 and VII7 in these quotations:

76

Secondary dominants may be replaced by diminished sevenths:

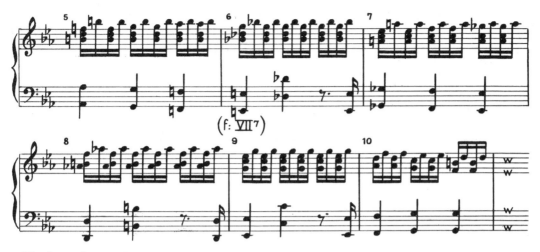

(f: $\underline{\text{VII}}^7$)

Keyboard practice

Transpose the above examples into other keys

The quotations from Schumann and Bach showed the expressive potential of a single diminished seventh built upon the sharpened subdominant.

Schumann   Bach

G: I   #IV♭7   V   a: I   #IV7   V

Used noisily, however, the chord can sound weak and melodramatic:

Allegro moderato, ma con fuoco   Mendelssohn, 'Elijah'

The wa-ters ga-ther, they rush a-long!   They are

lift - ing their voi - ces

How much more virile in *ff* is the *minor* seventh!

Mendelssohn, 'Midsummer Night's Dream' Music

Diminished sevenths are frequently found upon ♯II and ♯VI, as well as upon ♯IV. In this quotation from the 'Appassionata' sonata, for example, Beethoven links together the gentle, sustained, slow movement and the animated last movement by means of a diminished seventh chord. The chromatic chord of ♯II7 in the key of D♭ becomes the diatonic chord of VII7 (or 'V9 without the root') in F minor:

Beethoven, Sonata in F minor, Op.57

Since it follows many bars of mainly diatonic harmony, the progression II–V leads one to expect the usual I or VI. Instead, Beethoven writes ♯II7 which, in context, sounds strange indeed. No other chord is used for the ensuing twelve bars and it is only as the root of V9 in F minor takes a prominent position that the tonality begins to become clear.

The tonality of the diminished seventh chord is vague. When the chord is repeated the effect is of restlessness and uncertainty. This is because of the ambiguous nature of a chord which is capable of as many as forty-eight interpretations. We content ourselves with illustrating fourteen different resolutions and leave you to find some of the others.

Nos. 1–3 show the diatonic diminished seventh, VII7.
Nos. 4–7 show the diminished seventh used as a chromatic chord.
Nos. 2, 3 and 5 show enharmonic equivalents.

Since the diminished seventh consists of four superimposed minor thirds, all the inversions sound the same; compare nos. 1, 2, and 3.

Vivid and bewildering chains of diminished sevenths are to be found in the music of 19th-century Romantic composers:

Chopin, Etude, Op.10, N°3

The diminished seventh is at once the most versatile and the most ambiguous of chords, and has great histrionic potential. Skilfully used in the right context, it can induce feelings of wonder, awe, mystery, fear and restlessness, or the kind of delicate colouring that we found in the quotation from Schumann.

Keyboard practice
Analyse these progressions and play each one in several different keys.

Complete the following by introducing a diminished seventh or secondary dominant in each of the incomplete bars.

82

Complete the R.H. part from * in bar 5, maintaining the style of the previous bars and incorporating a number of diminished seventh chords.

Play and write passages of diatonic harmony and then substitute diminished sevenths in appropriate places, e.g.

Improvise short pieces based upon the chord progressions, e.g.

Poco scherzando

The Supertonic Chromatic Triad
The Supertonic Chromatic Seventh

These chords may be used as secondary dominants. When they function strictly as chromatic chords, the impression of a new leading note (F♯ in the following examples), is rebuffed by the V7 (F♮ here)) of the home key.

The supertonic chromatic chord is normally followed by V, Ic, VII, or VII7.

The supertonic chromatic seventh (similarly available in the minor mode).

The Neapolitan Sixth

This is the name given to the first inversion of the major triad built upon the flattened supertonic. The derivation from the Phrygian mode was explained in Chapter IV. The bass, being the only tonal degree, is the best note to double.

Play, sing, and analyse these progressions:

During the 19th century it became increasingly more usual to use the root position and this, curiously enough, is known as the 'Neapolitan Sixth in Root Position'.

The flattened supertonic degree is now treated as the true harmonic root and is doubled.

Notice that an augmented fourth or diminished fifth is involved when the bass moves to I_4^6 or to V.

Used at the very beginning of a movement, the Neapolitan sixth provides a solemn and momentous approach to dominant harmony. Compare these three impressive openings:

86

In the long sustained fugue subject that follows, notice the beautiful effect of the intervals of the augmented fourth, the minor second, and the diminished seventh, and of the lowered seventh and sixth degrees of the descending melodic minor scale. The first inversion of the chord of C acts as a pivot between E minor and B minor, being the diatonic VI6 in the former key, and the chromatic ♭II6 in the latter.

The striking character and arresting power of the Neapolitan sixth is further demonstrated in the opening of the 'Toreador's Song', where it follows the crashing dissonances of the V9 chords in the previous two bars:

Keyboard practice

Analyse carefully the progressions in the given examples and transpose each into at least one other key.

Continue the following sequence through the keys indicated:

Write chord progressions using the Neapolitan sixth,
(a) before the final cadence,
(b) at the beginning,
(c) as a pivot chord.
Examples:

88

Improvise short pieces based upon the chord progressions. Here are some suggestions for beginnings:

Augmented Sixth Chords

Do you recognize these harmonic progressions?

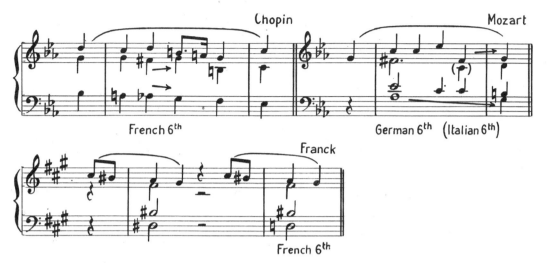

In each case the interval of the augmented sixth occurs between the bass and one of the upper parts and the chord proceeds to dominant harmony.

The 'Italian Sixth' evolves from the chromatic alteration of the root and third of chord IV, viz

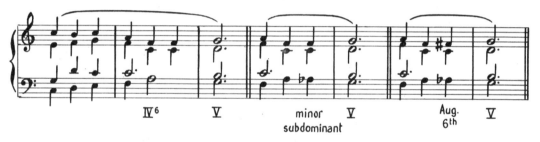

The 'German Sixth' contains the same notes as the 'Italian Sixth' with the addition of the diminished seventh from the root, viz

The consecutive perfect fifths arising in the resolution of the German Sixth are found either between the bass and tenor or between the bass and alto. They are avoided between the outer parts of the harmony.

The 'French Sixth' evolves from the chromatic alteration of II7.

90

We now show these three augmented sixth chords as they appear in the minor mode:

The following quotations include the use of the augmented sixth chords in very different contexts. The opening bars of Beethoven's 'Les Adieux' Sonata are deeply expressive, whilst those of the 'Thirty-two Variations' are heroic. The excerpt from Mozart's opera, *Così fan Tutte,* is gay and entertaining—you will enjoy choosing two soloists who can act their parts and catch the humour, and a pianist who is imaginative enough to do justice to the bustling 'um-char' bars, the sharp dramatic chords punctuating the exclamations, and the gentle, 'innocent' gavotte accompanying Despina.

Mozart, 'Cosi fan tutte'

In the next example occurs the unusual phenomenon of a 'German Sixth in Root Position'.

This passage comes at the end of the long, sorrowful 'Crucifixus', in which a throbbing ground bass, involving descending semitones in the key of E minor, has been heard twelve times.

92

During the thirteenth and final appearance it is adjusted to lead to a cadence in the relative major key. It is on the root of the German sixth chord (C♯) that the change occurs.

All voices descend to the lowest notes of their registers and a sense of overwhelming grief is felt.

Sing the whole of the 'Crucifixus' and study the wonderful use of chromatic harmony, expressive intervals and poignant suspensions in this tragically intense movement. Listen to a recording of the 'Crucifixus' followed by the blaze of jubilant exhilaration in the 'Et resurrexit'.

Keyboard practice
Carefully analyse and transpose the given examples.
Write and play chord progressions involving Augmented sixth chords.
Improvise short characteristic pieces.

Here are two simple examples for practice in transposition:

Identify these chromatic chords and then experiment with different chords of approach and resolution. Incorporate each chord in a musical sentence.

Explore the use of chromatic harmony by the great masters of the 18th and 19th centuries. As possible models for your creative work you might study in particular the recitatives in Mozart's operas, the slow movements of sonatas by Haydn, Mozart, Beethoven, and Schubert, and some of the hundreds of exquisite miniatures to be found amongst such pieces as:

Beethoven	*Bagatelles*
Schumann	*Album for the Young; Scenes from Childhood; Papillons; Carnaval; Kreisleriana.*
Chopin	*Mazurkas*
Grieg	*Lyric Pieces*
Mendelssohn	*Songs without Words*
Tchaikovsky	*Album for the Young*
Brahms	*Capricci* and *Intermezzi*

For a fuller exposition of chromatic harmony, consult the *Oxford Harmony*

94

Book Two, by H. K. Andrews, *Harmony* by Walter Piston (Gollancz) and *The Oxford School Harmony Course,* Book Two, by James Denny.

In the late 19th century German composers such as Wolf, Wagner, and Richard Strauss developed chromaticism to such an extent that the traditional prominence of the tonic and dominant began to be challenged. The process continued until Schoenberg, in the early 1920s, discovered that in some of his compositions all twelve notes of the chromatic scale were of equal importance. Students wishing to study the twelve-note system are recommended to begin with Smith Brindle's *Serial Composition* (OUP), Rufer's *Composition with twelve notes* (Rockliff) and Humphrey Searle's *20th Century Counterpoint* (Benn).

The evolution of the harmonic writing of the French Impressionists, notably Fauré, Debussy, Ravel, and Koechlin, may be traced in *A Study of 20th Century Harmony,* Volume I, by René Lenormand (Joseph Williams).

In the present chapter we have been chiefly concerned to show the most usual procedures of the classical and romantic composers of the 18th and early 19th centuries. We conclude with another quotation from *Così fan Tutte* for you to sing—diminished seventh, augmented sixth, and Neapolitan chords are all to be found.

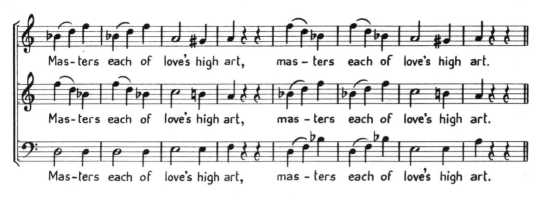

Mas-ters each of love's high art, mas-ters each of love's high art.

Mas-ters each of love's high art, mas-ters each of love's high art.

Mas-ters each of love's high art, mas-ters each of love's high art.

CHAPTER SEVEN

CONTRAPUNTAL WRITING IN TWO AND THREE PARTS

Sing and play this extract from *Don Giovanni*.

In Act II, Scene 3, from which this passage is taken, Don Giovanni and his servant Leporello are lurking in a graveyard which contains a statue in memory of the Commendatore who was killed in a duel by Don Giovanni. It is midnight, and as the two men relate their adventures they are suddenly startled when the statue comes to life and issues a solemn warning to Don Giovanni. Giovanni is undismayed: he coolly invites the statue to supper. When the statue accepts this mocking invitation Leporello is terrified, but Don Giovanni remains unperturbed.

Notice Mozart's skilful characterization. Giovanni's unruffled urbanity is shown by a legato melody moving mainly in crotchets, while Leporello's agitation is revealed by the patter of staccato quavers. In the orchestra, violins play a stream of semiquavers which add to the general excitement and emphasize Leporello's impatience to be off. These three strands of melody combine in effortless counterpoint, and because of their rhythmic independence, each stands out clearly in performance. The harmonies used are simple. Dissonance and imitation are not employed. Our interest is engaged by the rhythmic counterpoint and we enjoy the effect produced by contrasted rhythms in opposition.

The ability to write flowing parts in contrasting rhythms is one of the first requirements of contrapuntal technique, and two-part writing is especially useful for the opportunity it affords to develop this skill.

Add a bass part which moves in crotchets. Halt the movement on the last note of each line.

1.
Slow and solemn   'Valet will ich dir geben' (S. P. 135)

Here is the first part of a Minuet, beginning in B♭ and modulating to the dominant. Complete the melody, maintaining the quaver movement until the final bar.

2.

Complete the bass part in the following passage. We have indicated the places where Mendelssohn abandons octaves for single notes, and also the one occasion when he uses repeated notes. The rest of the passage is in the style of the opening bars and quaver movement is maintained throughout.

3.

The next example is from Bach's cantata No. 140, 'Wachet auf', and the part you are asked to complete is taken from the oboe 'obbligato' in the sixth movement. Maintain the semiquaver movement and let the melody rise to a graceful climax in the third bar.

4.

Allegro moderato

J.S. Bach, 'Sleepers Wake!'

Begin as follows :—

Here is a quotation from Handel's well-known 'Air and Variations' in E major. Complete the bass part, keeping up an unbroken flow of triplet semiquavers as far as *.

The opening motif (a) predominates until half-way through the fourth bar, when it gives way to different melodic patterns, and we have indicated the two most important of these.

5.

Allegro

Handel, Suite N⁰ V in E

Some melodic patterns to consider:

Add a bass part that moves in quavers throughout

a) G minor   b) C minor

Begin as follows:

(Add phrasing and dynamics).

Complete the bass part in the following passage from Beethoven. We have indicated places where the part halts. For the remainder of the time there is an unbroken flow of semiquavers

So far we have been considering contrasted rhythms in combination and, particularly, the effect produced when one part moves evenly at a different speed to another. We now turn our attention to a second kind of rhythmic interplay.

Very commonly, two or more parts in a musical texture are based on one rhythmical pattern, but by entering at different times, and so overlapping, the parts assert their independence and generate tension.

Here is the rhythm of 'Au clair de la lune':

A second part, adopting this rhythm, but entering one bar later than the tune, provides an effective counterpoint, and the result is a rhythmic canon.

When two parts share a rhythm they usually share the tune also, the second part imitating the first.

Let us complete a two-part arrangement of 'Au clair de la lune'. We reflect on the melodic ideas that we might use in our second part.

102

We remember that 'imitation' implies freedom to modify. There is no merit in trying to enforce strict repetition of a phrase if the result is poor harmony and awkward part-writing. It is much wiser to modify the 'point'.

Here is a two-part arrangement of 'Searching for Lambs'.

Notice that the parts cross in the opening phrase. Do not hesitate to cross the parts in your own writing when by so doing you are able to give your phrases point and shapeliness. You will have noticed examples of inversion in both arrangements. Make a habit of singing mentally the inversions of the themes you employ. Inversions bring variety, and at times when direct imitation is impossible they afford a means of bringing significance to a part that might otherwise be aimless.

Here is a selection of tunes that lend themselves to the kind of treatment that we have been discussing. As you make your two-part arrangements,

think in terms of particular instruments. Nos. 2–5 might well be for brass—
Nos. 6–9 for strings or woodwind. Whatever instruments you decide upon,
remember to add suitable phrasing and dynamics.

Now that we have attempted two forms of rhythmic independence, one based on contrast, the other on imitation, it is time to carry our investigations a stage further and examine a movement in which both kinds of counterpoint are employed.

106

Here is the first part of the Allemande from Bach's French Suite in B minor:

Points to observe:

Rhythm	*Imitation* determines the pattern in bars 1, 5, 6, 7, 10, and 11.

        Contrast predominates in bars 2, 3, 4, and 9.

        Notice particularly the way in which the two effects are mingled. The music never settles into square-cut periods. We are pleasurably intrigued as it unfolds, unable to be sure of the course it will take, and because of this element of suspense the total effect is one of spontaneity and freshness.

Melody   The opening motif (a) is present in some form or other in practically every bar. (In which bar does it not appear?)

        Notice the modifications that it undergoes. The opening interval of a perfect fourth becomes a sixth at (b) and a seventh at (e), and these are only two of the changes. Find an augmented fourth, a diminished fifth, a perfect fifth, a minor sixth, and a diminished seventh.

        Notice the inversion (c) in bars 2, 3, and 4.

        Notice, too, the way in which the last note of the motif varies in length in different passages.

Harmonic rhythm   Four harmonies per measure is the normal practice here, but monotony is avoided by occasional departures from this, e.g. quaver harmonies on the last beat of bar 5 as the D major section is rounded-off with a perfect cadence. (Notice that this cadence does not interrupt the flow of the music: the upper part maintains its semi-quaver movement.)

        Occasionally a harmony lasts longer than a beat, e.g. the diminished seventh on the last beat of bar 8 is carried on until the second beat of bar 9.

General   Play each part separately and enjoy the shapeliness of the melodic lines. Notice the constant rise and fall and the fluctuations in tension. (What is the over-all direction of the melody?).

        Notice the key scheme:

Tonic	Relative Major	Dominant
b	D	f♯

        Notice, too, the four-part harmony in the final bar, enriching the cadence and pointing the form.

Complete the Allemande by adding a bass part. We have indicated Bach's rhythm. Compare your version with the original and discuss with your tutor.

B minor

Add bass parts to the following.

1.

Menuetto

J.S. Bach, Brandenburg Concerto Nº 1

oboe

mp

Begin as follows:-

mp

2.

Presto   Mozart, K.504 'Prague' Symphony

Write a short duo in two-part form for horns in F. We have provided a rhythmic outline for the first eight bars. Let the second player lead at the beginning of the second part.

3.

Andante

Horns in F sound a fifth lower than written:

Tempo di Menuetto   Beethoven, Symphony N°8

sounding

Normal working compass:

Write a duo for piano based on the following rhythms:

4.

Andante pastorale

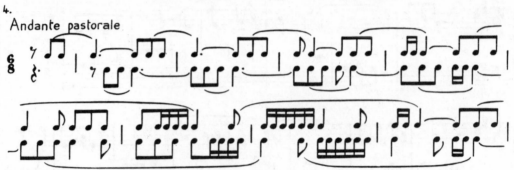

The movement that follows is from a trio-sonata by Corelli. It should be performed in various ways. Begin by playing it on the piano, which will be useful practice in score-reading. Then organize a trio performance. The upper parts may be played by string or wind instruments, according to the resources of your group. The continuo player should extemporize an accompaniment from the figured bass. Listen carefully as you rehearse and note the characteristics of this style of writing.

Notice the contrapuntal nature of the two principal parts: they move independently for most of the time; imitation predominates and phrases overlap. Counterpoint gives way to harmony for a brief spell in bars 13–17 as the two violins play together in thirds. This touch of contrast adds to the effectiveness of the imitative writing when it returns.

Ask yourself what you can learn from this passage with regard to the crossing of parts, the use of rests and the maintenance of flow at cadence points.

Here are two further passages in similar style. Complete the parts for Violin II, bearing in mind the implications of the figured bass.

1.

2.

Grave

Corelli, Sonata da chiesa Op.3, N°7

The next example comes from a fine duet from Purcell's *Diocletian*. Complete the second soprano part—we have indicated Purcell's rhythm.

More tunes for contrapuntal treatment

Write in two or three parts as seems most appropriate. Devise arrangements that are varied in style and be resourceful in your choice of instruments and voices. Transpose the tunes to suit your requirements.

6. Vivo — 'The Jolly Miller'

rit. a tempo

7. Andante — Coventry Carol (O C.B.)

8. Giocoso — 'Alouette'

9. Moderato — English Folk Song

Come all you wild young peo - ple and lis - ten to _ my song, While
I will un-fold con - cer-ning gold, That guides so ma-ny wrong. Young
Em-ma was a ser-vant maid, And _ loved a sail - or bold. He
ploughed the main, much gold to gain for his love, as we've been told.

10. Allegro giocoso — 'Come ye not from Newcastle'

11. **Andante sostenuto** — English Folk Carol (OCB 68)

mp

This is the truth sent from a-bove, The truth of God, — the God of love, There-fore don't turn me — from your door, But hear-ken all — both — rich and poor. —

12. **Con spirito** — Scottish Air

13. **Andante semplice** — 'Greensleeves'

Complete the following extract by continuing the tenor part. The passage comes from one of Thomas Morley's *Canzonets to Two Voices*. Study these compositions carefully and arrange performances with your friends.

14. 'Rather slow — Morley, Canzonet

mf

Sop.

Leave now mine eyes la-ment - - - ing, your tears, your

mf

Ten.

Leave now mine eyes la-ment - - -

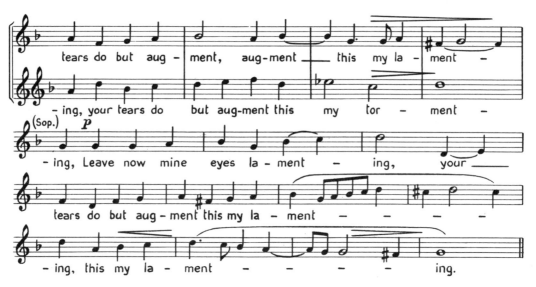

Complete the following by continuing the first violin part. Maintain the style of the opening bars. Consult the original when you have completed your working and refer to Chapter Nine as you explore the variations that comprise the second movement of this famous quartet (Op. 76, No. 3).

15.

Complete the left hand part of this Passepied by Bach. Two-part writing is maintained throughout. Notice the rondo form (ABACA).

118

16

Allegro vivo

Bach, Passepied I *from*
English Suite N°5

CHAPTER EIGHT

CHORALES

J. S. Bách attained a wonderful expressiveness in his treatment of chorales. A study of his methods is invaluable in developing one's understanding and interpretation of music.

We assume that by now you will have had considerable experience of choral singing and have rehearsed some of Bach's Passion music and cantatas. Perhaps, however, you are more vividly aware of the part you normally sing than of the other three voices. Be sure to sing each voice part in turn (transposing an octave where necessary) of the examples you study and write.

Decide how true are the following generalizations when applied to individual chorales:

1. The simple chorale melodies are ornamented by passing, auxiliary and anticipatory notes (a).

a,   b, d, j,   e, h

2. Alto lines may sometimes *look* dull, but careful attention to interpretation reveals great expressive potential.
3. Tenor parts are intensely beautiful. High notes are a feature.
4. Bass parts are wide-ranging and impressive.
5. Prepared suspensions (often sevenths) are preferred to appoggiaturas and are very common, especially in the alto and tenor parts. (b)
6. The chord of the diminished seventh occurs as VII7 in the minor mode and chromatically as ♯IV7. (c) It is also to be found in secondary dominant effects. (u)

c,   g, j,   i

7. A characteristic use of chromatic harmony is ♯II⁶₅–V7–I at phrase-endings. (d)
8. The Tierce de Picardie brings sweet repose at a final cadence. (e)
9. Chord changes occur on nearly every beat. Sometimes, however, Bach uses the same chord for two or three beats and this occasionally from a weaker to a stronger accent. (f)

   A clinging effect is obtained by changing chords on half-beats. (g)

a, f, a,   a, b,

10. In the inner parts of chorales, Bach frequently drops the leading note to the fifth of the tonic chord (h) or takes it up to the third. (i) This procedure denies the leading note its usual tendency but ensures a complete final chord.
11. Extraordinary spacing arises. (j)
12. Parts may overlap, especially between the ending of one line and the commencement of the next. (k)

l, k,   a, f,   u, b,   b, j,   b,   h, e

13. One part may 'run-in' to another—a choral effect comparable to 'heavy pedalling' on the pianoforte. (l)
14. Consecutive fifths separated by a subsidiary harmony note, (m) fifths by contrary motion, (n) and fifths interrupted by a suspension (o) or caused by a note of anticipation (p) are not uncommon.

a,   b,   n, k, r,   t, l, k, b,   m

o

15. An exposed 8ve (the two outer parts of the harmony move in the same direction towards an 8ve, the upper part leaping), (q) and 8ves by contrary motion (r) are occasionally to be found.

16. Parts frequently cross (s) and the bass of the first inversion of the major triad is doubled. (t)

The idiosyncracies noted in paragraphs 11 to 16 arise because Bach has allowed the melodic interest in the four voices to prevail, notwithstanding the resultant unconventional harmony. George Oldroyd used to say that Bach's attitude towards the relative importance of harmony and counterpoint might be compared with that of a king and his queen: the king (harmony) normally has precedence, but he may sometimes forego his prerogative and allow the queen (counterpoint) pre-eminence for a short time!

The quotations so far have been taken from the *Passion according to St. Matthew*. Study carefully all the chorales in this work and identify the phrases we have used.

Now consider the first chorale in the *Passion according to St. John*, a fine example of a treatment that is consistently interesting both harmonically and melodically. Notice the magnificent contours and the telling use of a wide range of pitch in each of the four voices:

122

(1) The impressive harmonization—I–IV7–II$_3^{4}$^{6}—of the repeated tonic note is followed by chords of the dominant or leading note and tonic only for the remainder of the phrase. This firmly establishes the key prior to the chromaticism of the next two phrases.

(2) The seventh is prepared.

(3) VII6 (the first inversion of the diminished triad on the leading note) is nearly always preferred to V$_4^{6}$ (the 'Passing $_4^{6}$').

(4) VII7, the diatonic diminished seventh. Find another example.

(5) 'Run-in'. Find another example.

(6) Unconventional treatment of the leading note in V$_4^{6}$–I6.

(7) Doubled bass of first inversion of a major triad.

(8) Note the effect of 'walking' and 'sadness' in the chromatically descending crotchets.

(9) An unusual use of the $_4^{6}$ chord.

(10) ♯II$_5^{6}$ (The D♭ is an accented chromatic passing note). Find another example of ♯II$_5^{6}$.

(11) A prepared suspension. Find another example.

(12) The leading note falls to complete the tonic chord. Find another example.

(13) The diminished seventh used as a transition chord to the key of D minor.

(14) The Continuo is shown in small notes where it differs from the vocal bass. What effect would its omission have in this phrase?

(15) Unusually close harmony. Note the clash of the minor second suspension.

(16) Tierce de Picardie.

Write careful notes on the two chorales that follow:

All glo-ry, laud, and ho - nour To Thee Re-dee-mer, King.
To whom the lips of chil - dren Made sweet ho-san-nas ring. *FINE*

Thou art the King of Is - rael, Thou Da-vid's roy-al Son,

Who in the Lord's name com - eth, The King and bles-sèd one.

D.C. al fine

C. S. Terry's edition (OUP) of some 400 chorales harmonized by J. S. Bach affords an excellent study.

There are also some 83 hymn tunes, with a bass, either used or wholly composed by Bach, to be found in Schemelli's hymn book, the *Notenbuch* prepared for Anna Magdalena Bach, and in a manuscript of Bach's pupil J. L. Krebs. Complete the following examples for four voices in the style you think Bach might have adopted. (We give suggested dynamics, in place of words, in some of the examples and leave you to decide the interpretation in others). Compare your solutions with those of the great choral conductor Charles Kennedy Scott, to be found in *Fifty Sacred Songs by J. S. Bach* (OUP).

In writing down the examples, do not copy individual notes separately, but memorize a phrase at a time and sing as you write.

4. Con giubilo

5. Andante cantabile

126

Many passages reminiscent of the chorale are to be found in the music of the 19th and 20th centuries. As well as obvious specimens, such as the chorale in Mendelssohn's oratorio *St. Paul,* we find instrumental music evoking comparable feelings. Little adjustment, for example, is needed to change the style from pianistic to vocal and thereby evince a chorale mood in this extract from a 'Song without Words' by Mendelssohn.

Consult the following works and find other examples:

Schumann	*Album for the Young*
Chopin	*Preludes*
Mendelssohn	*Prelude and Fugue in E minor,* Op. 35, No. 1
Brahms	*Rhapsodie* for Alto Solo, Male Chorus and Orchestra, Op. 53
Wagner	*Lohengrin*
Franck	*Prelude, Chorale and Fugue*
Saint-Saëns	*Pianoforte Concerto No. 4*
Bartók	*Concerto for Orchestra*
Berg	*Violin Concerto*
Britten	*St. Nicolas*
Tippett	*A Child of Our Time*

128

Here are two more chorales for you to sing:

Sehr lang und gleichmässig stark ausgehalten

A - wake! The dawn of day draws near: From deep-est

woods I hear A soul-glad-den-ing nightin-gale; His voice sounds o'er hill and

The night des-cends the west-ern sky And from the east the

The night des-cends the west-ern sky And morn from the
The night leaves the west-ern sky And from the east the

dale _____ And from the east the

morn draws nigh, With red ar - dour the flush of day Breaks

morn draws nigh, With red ar - dour the flush of day
morn draws nigh, With red ar - dour the flush of day Breaks

morn draws nigh, With red ar - dour the flush of day Breaks

130

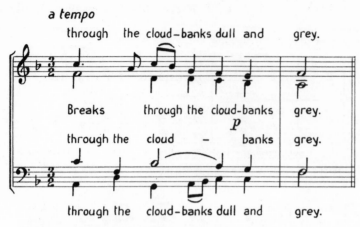

The action of *The Mastersingers* takes place in the Germany of the 16th
century! 'Wagner', writes Alfred Einstein in *Music in the Romantic Era*
(W. W. Norton), 'utilized the style of Bach with a violence that was in keeping
with his natural propensities for conquest. Completely disregarding the
anachronism of his approach, he introduced the polyphony of Bach in place
of 16th-century music. In so doing he secured a point of contrast with his
own personal tonal language, without giving up a bit of his own individuality
in the very act of imitation.'

CHAPTER NINE

VARIATIONS

In Chapter Four we indicated various ways of treating this nursery tune:

Try to recreate these styles at the piano and then refer back to our versions:
1. 'Giocoso'—add a sprightly L.H. part, using only the simplest diatonic harmony.
2. 'Espressivo'—a smooth, three-part version, with a more interesting harmonic rhythm and a glimpse of C major in bar 2.
3. 'Maestoso'—a four-part chorale, with a firm cadence in C major in bar 2.
4. 'Dolce'—play from memory the Czech carol 'Little Jesus'. (Between the first and last phrases is interpolated a repetition of bar 2. The musical sentence is one of five bars.)

Complete the following and then experiment with other styles:

Think of some other folk and composed melodies closely resembling this nursery tune—several have been used in these two books.

Listen to and comment upon:

Variations on 'Ah! vous dirai-je, Maman'   Mozart, K.265
Le Carnaval des animaux   Saint-Saëns
Variations on a nursery theme   Dohnanyi

Simple melodies based upon scales have proved effective as a basis for variations.

Play the scale of G descending:

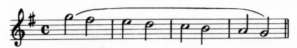

Change the octave of the first two bars and repeat some of the notes:

Ornament with échappées, passing notes, and a suspension:

Add octaves in the announcing phrase and simple harmony in the responsive phrase: the result is the first sentence of the Air, 'Unser dummer Pobel meint' from Gluck's opera *Pilgrims of Mecca* as used by Mozart in his Variations, K.455 (Augener Edition No. 8251B).

Bars 5–8 consist of a modulating sequence in the supertonic minor and tonic keys. Name the chords used. In bars 9–12 the original sentence is repeated '*f*'.

In variation 1, the melody is decorated with a profusion of passing notes, auxiliary notes, appoggiaturas, etc., so that the R.H. part is almost continuously in semiquavers. Write and play the missing semiquavers in the following incomplete version and then compare your solution with the original.

Similarly, complete with triplets in the graceful variation 3:

134

In Variation 7 Mozart provides a colourful harmonization in which each of
the five most closely related keys are briefly touched upon.

Name the keys and chords and point out pivot chords and sequences.

Notice, too, the artistic use made of the ♪♫ rhythm which decorates
the responsive phrases.

VAR. 7

Variation 10 begins with the following delightful version of the scale, this
time in 3/8 :

VAR. 10

Allegro

Try your hand at continuing this opening and making a satisfying return to
the original tempo and rhythm for a final statement of the theme and a short
coda.

Make a careful study of the complete work and discuss each variation
with your tutor or fellow-students.

We now quote briefly from the *Leichte Variationem* (Toccata) of Dimitri
Kabalewski, Op. 40, No. 1 (Edition Peters No. 4707).

Again the theme is based upon the descending major scale which, after a
brief Prelude, is heard divided between two octaves.

Allegretto brioso

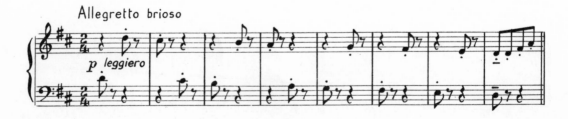

Each of the first three Variations is a terse eight-bar sentence in which the scale appears in the L.H. punctuated by quavers in the R.H.

Complete these three sentences at the piano, maintaining the lively style.

Improvise some variations of your own before studying Kabalewski's Toccata. Here are suggestions:
1. Dramatic or humorous distortions of rhythm and contrasts of dynamics.
2. A 'Dolce' variation with triplets, or an 'Appassionata' movement in which the theme is temporarily forgotten.
3. A brilliant finale.

The Toccata is most effective as a concert piece, yet is not very difficult to play. You would also enjoy Kabalewski's *Five Easy Variations,* Op. 51 (Anglo-Soviet Music Press), which are based upon Russian, Slovakian, and Ukrainian folk-songs.

We now draw your attention to the very fine set of variations which forms the first movement of Michael Tippett's Piano Sonata No. 1 (Schott Edition No. 10123). It is recorded by Margaret Kitchin (Lyrita RCS5).

Once more we find the descending scale, this time beginning on *s* and continuing down to *m,* but omitting *r.* All but the last of these notes are syncopated.

Notice also, that—
1. As the melody unfolds, particular notes are picked out from it to build a chord which at first seems to be V7 but in bar 4 becomes more akin to IV. It progresses quietly to I.
2. Each bar is divided into two unequal parts, $\frac{3}{4}+\frac{2}{4}$. The effect at first is angular and arresting, but, in bar 4 this impression fades and the unusual compound of triple and duple rhythms proves compatible with the beautiful cantabile style of bars 5–9.

Allegro

136

Let four students sing this passage while another plays the L.H. quavers of bars 5–9.

The strident style of the first bars returns in bar 9 to be contrasted in bar 10 with quiet flowing quavers derived from the accompaniment of bars 5–8.

A similar contrast occurs in bars 11 and 12.

Bar 13 begins similarly, but, in this third limb of the sequence, a development occurs—the $\frac{3}{4}+\frac{2}{4}$ idea is expanded to $\frac{3}{4}+\frac{3}{4}$.

There follows a return to $\frac{3}{4}+\frac{2}{4}$ and a quiet plagal cadence.

Bars 17–25 are similar to bars 9–16, but consistent quaver movement is maintained. As the R.H. returns to the sequential idea, the L.H. accompanies with legato quavers. In bar 18, however, the L.H. is grouped in $\frac{3}{8}+\frac{2}{8}+\frac{3}{8}+\frac{2}{8}$ while the R.H. has $\frac{3}{4}+\frac{2}{4}$.

In bars 19 and 20 the sequence is continued, again with the new interest in the L.H. rhythm.

Contrary motion and the use of a wide range of pitch contribute to a big crescendo in the $\frac{3}{4}+\frac{3}{4}$ bars:

ff is reached and this, combined with strong accentuation, a *ritard.,* and a long final chord, gives power and finality to the plagal cadence.

The first variation begins with a sparkling figuration based upon a $\frac{3}{4} + \frac{5}{8}$ rhythm—

In bar 4 this is extended by the addition of a second group of 5 quavers—$\frac{3}{4} + \frac{5}{8} + \frac{5}{8}$.

This leads to a quiet, expressive passage based upon $\frac{4}{4} + \frac{3}{8}$.

Listen many times to this variation and discover other rhythmic groupings within it.

There follows a vigorous contrapuntal movement in which melodic and rhythmic derivations are easy to find.

The sparse, thin harmony and fierce syncopation act as a foil to the grand, chorale style of Variation 3, with its solid $\frac{4}{4}$ and impressive span of more than five octaves of the keyboard.

In Variation 4 a return is made to two-part writing, this time in a sprightly, scherzando style. A perky tune, based upon the major scale and first heard high up in the treble, occurs again and again at different pitches above or below a somewhat similar motif written in invertible counterpoint. The jerky, dotted rhythm is heard hundreds of times, only occasionally relieved by an angular syncopated idea.

The last variation begins with an ominous and restless motif in the style of the gamelan music of Bali.

Consult the score to trace the original theme, now based upon the minor scale.

The *pp* is dramatically disturbed by violent crescendi which lead to short bursts of *f* and *ff*. The final crescendo develops to a consistent *ff* which culminates brilliantly in a triumphant restatement of the original theme.

Remarkable flexibility of rhythm is also a notable feature of Tippett's exhilarating Concerto for Double String Orchestra, (Schott Edition No. 5146; recorded by the Moscow Chamber Orchestra and the Bath Festival Chamber Orchestra, ALP 1961). Explore the diversity obtained
(a) by varying the position of the rhythmic accents to produce two equal or three unequal beats in bars of $\frac{8}{8}$

(b) by alternating between $\frac{3}{4}$ and $\frac{6}{8}$

(c) by changing time signatures.

Projects

1. Explore variations by other composers from the Elizabethans to the present day.
2. Plan a programme to be performed by members of your group.
3. Devise an interesting series of record recitals tracing variations through the centuries.
4. Write a comprehensive list of technical devices used in variations and be able to quote examples.
5. Choose or compose your own theme and write a set of variations.
6. Use variation techniques in setting songs.

Notice that themes chosen are usually simple in structure. Harmonize each of the following at the piano and then sketch or improvise six or seven possible variations. Finally look up the original composition, play and discuss. You may find that members of your group devise some excellent variants quite unlike any that occurred to the original composer!

Sing these five songs several times and decide upon interpretation and instrumentation. 'A Cossack Lullaby', for example, might be set for voice, piano, and *either* clarinet *or* bassoon:

Verse 1 Voice with a simple piano accompaniment.

Verse 2 Theme played by clarinet or bassoon while voice sings a simple counterpoint; piano silent.

Verse 3 Re-introduce the piano during the long final note of Verse 2. Use a sturdy, sonorous texture.

Verse 4 Obtain a stretto effect by means of a steady increase in complexity of scoring and an accelerando.

Verse 5 A maestoso version in the tonic major.

Be sure to compose artistic links between the stanzas and to introduce and rest instruments with care; the counterpoint sung in Verse 2 might serve as the basis of an instrumental introduction to Verse 1; a brilliant cadenza might be developed after Verse 4 and culminate in a Tierce de Picardie for the commencement of Verse 5.

A Cossack Lullaby

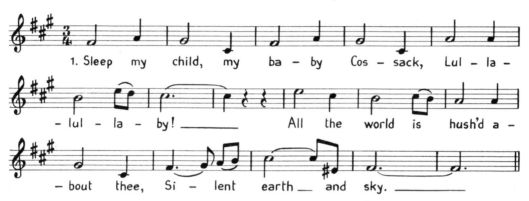

1. Sleep my child, my ba-by Cos-sack, Lul-la-lul-la-by! All the world is hush'd a-bout thee, Si-lent earth and sky.

2 'Mid the snow the wolves are howling
   Lulla-lulla-by,
 Through the dark, bright eyes are shining
   Watchful there they lie.
3 Strong thy father's arm to guard thee,
   Lulla-lulla-by,
 Safe thy home in father's keeping,
   Sleep till break of day.

4 Mother's hands shall deck his saddle,
   Lulla-lulla-by,
 Mother's heart shall bless his going,
   When he rides away.
5 Proudly mother's eyes shall watch him,
   Lulla-lulla-by,
 Ne'er was seen so brave a Cossack
   On his charger high.

King Herod and the Cock

Not too slow   (OBC 54)

There was a star in Da-vid's land, So bright it did ap-pear In-to King He-rod's cham-ber, And bright-ly it shined there.

2 The Wise Men soon espied it,
   And told the king on high,
 A princely babe was born that night
   No king could e'er destroy.

3 'If this be true,' King Herod said,
   'As thou hast told to me,
 This roasted cock that lies in the dish
   Shall crow full fences three.'

4 The cock soon thrustened and feathered well,
   By the work of God's own hand,
 And he did crow full fences three,
   In the dish where he did stand.

(*fences:* times; *thrustened:* thrust out)

144

My Little Donkey

Folk-tune from Orléannais

Words by Helen Henschel

1. I love my lit-tle don-key, Hee haw, ___ Hee haw, ___ I
love my lit-tle don-key, His coat's so soft, His vel-vet coat's so soft. ___

2 I drive my little donkey,
Gee up, Gee up,
I drive my little donkey
In a painted cart,
A little painted cart.

3 The bells they jingle gaily,
Ding dong, ding dong,
The bells they jingle gaily
As off we trot,
Merrily off we trot.

4 I lead my little donkey
Hee haw, Hee haw,
I lead my little donkey
To bed in his stall,
So good night, that's all.

She's like the Swallow

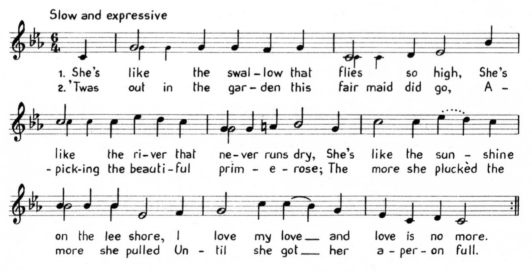

1. She's like the swal-low that flies so high, She's
like the ri-ver that ne-ver runs dry, She's like the sun - shine
on the lee shore, I love my love ___ and love is no more.

2. 'Twas out in the gar-den this fair maid did go, A-
-pick-ing the beauti-ful prim - e - rose; The more she plucked the
more she pulled Un - til she got ___ her a - per-on full.

3 It's out of those roses she made a bed,
A stony pillow for her head.
She laid her down, no word did say,
Until this fair maid's heart did break.

4 She's like the swallow that flies so high,
She's like the river that never runs dry,
She's like the sunshine on the lee shore,
I love my love and love is no more.

Christmas Carol from Somerset

The lit-tle young lambs were on the hill. Glo - ry, Glo - ry. The

night was cold and the wind it was still. Glo-ry,Glo - ry, Glo - ry. They

look-èd high, they look-èd low, But all they saw was a star in the sky.

Sing - ing Glo - ry, Glo - ry, Glo - ry, Christ is born.

Add in last verse only

Christ is born, Christ is born.

2 They lookèd low, they lookèd high, Glory, Glory.
There came a great light into the sky, Glory, Glory, Glory.
And all God's angels sang out plain
So sweet as collybirds after rain.
Singing, 'Glory, Glory, Glory, Christ is born'.

3 Go little young lambs to Bethlehem, Glory, Glory.
And there you will find the King of men, Glory, Glory, Glory.
In the manger on the hay
The lamb that's born on Chrissimas day.
Singing, 'Glory, Glory, Glory, Christ is born'.

4 The little young lambs away they went, Glory, Glory.
And followed their shepherds in great content, Glory, Glory, Glory.
And in a manger there he lay.
Our Lord was born on Chrissimas Day.
Singing, 'Glory, Glory, Glory, Christ is born'.
'Christ is born, Christ is born'.

(Collected by Michael Bell, 1959)

Now try your skill at the composition, rehearsal and performance of an
Operetta, a Missa Brevis or a more extended work suited to the capabilities
of the singers and players at your disposal.

APPENDIX ON EXAMINATIONS

Students should obtain the current syllabus of any examination they wish to sit and copies of the most recent papers. Examining boards modify their requirements and style of question from time to time.

THE GENERAL CERTIFICATE OF EDUCATION
ORDINARY LEVEL
Harmony in Four Parts

The added parts must maintain the style of the given passage.

Soprano and bass must have melodic interest and a good balance between contrary, similar and oblique motion.

Alto and tenor parts should have melodic interest as far as possible. Remember that careful attention to rhythm and dynamics can bring point to a line that is severely restricted in range of pitch.

A convention established in elementary examinations is that certain intervals are 'awkward' to sing and to be avoided melodically. Such are the major seventh and all augmented intervals. The following examples are regarded as 'unvocal':

The note that follows a leap of a minor seventh or any diminished interval should be within that interval. The following, for example, are 'correct':

A candidate who writes consecutive unisons or octaves (or an octave preceded or followed by a unison) is thereby reducing the number of real parts and avoiding the issue of harmony in four parts.

The 'exposed 8ve' and 'exposed fifth' (the two outer parts moving in the same direction to an 8ve or fifth, the upper part leaping) are similarly unacceptable.

A further prohibition is of consecutive perfect fifths which are said to disturb the tonality.

There is no such objection to consecutive unequal fifths (a perfect fifth preceded or followed by a diminished fifth) when, as in the following progressions, the lowest moving part is not involved:

We now consider questions set in recent years by the Welsh Joint Education Committee.

'Complete the following for SATB. Modulate to the dominant at the end of the first phrase.'

(W.J.E.C. 1961)

Read the instructions carefully; mentally sing through the given phrases several times; decide upon the general style and upon keys and cadences. No indications of tempo or dynamics are given, so these must be chosen by the candidate. A steady, dignified style seems appropriate for the opening phrase whilst the responsive phrase, with its confident rising quavers and repeated high dominant, needs to be equally broad and perhaps more emphatic. We therefore pencil in possible solutions for the cadences and interpretation:

Contrary motion seems obvious at the beginning of each phrase.

Leading note—tonic in the bass indicates V6–I or V_5^6–I.

In harmonizing the second degree of the scale we have three possibilities:

(a) the first inversion of the diminished triad,

(b) the 'rising seventh',   or (c) the 'passing $\frac{6}{4}$'

We reject (a) and (b) because the alto part is weak. In (c) the alto part is correct but dull.

We notice also an exposed fifth and a feeble tenor part. Both these latter criticisms may be answered by rearranging the notes of the cadence:

This solution is satisfactory.

Since the leading note E♮ is in an inner part we may, if we wish, allow it to fall to C and thus complete the chord of F major. A further slight adjustment of the inner parts improves the range and interest of both alto and tenor:

148

This version will prove particularly apt if we are able to include a similar syncopation in the responsive phrase.

In returning to the tonic key, chord I in F becomes V in B♭.

We now add a syncopated alto part and a tenor part that continues the quaver movement inaugurated by the soprano. The high notes of the alto and tenor and the wide spacing between tenor and bass contribute to the climax in the dynamics.

Alternatively, by changing the bass and abandoning the syncopation, we may improve the contrapuntal interest.

Compare these two completed solutions:

We suggest a figured bass which you may use at your discretion in working this similar exercise:

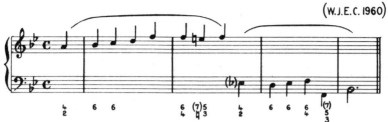

The next question is more interesting, as so many harmonizations are possible.

'Complete this fragment, adapted from a motet attributed to Richard Farrant, for four-part choir.'

The B♮ indicates a modulation to the dominant or to the relative minor of the dominant.

Compare the following arrangements of the Imperfect Cadence required at the end of the first phrase:

There is more interest in the alto and tenor parts of (b) and (d) than in those of (a) and (c). Harmonically, however, (e) is preferable, since here the bass avoids the important dominant note just before the cadence.

In this slow-moving passage some activity under the first minim is desirable. We may proceed from root position to first inversion, or vice versa, of the same chord, or we may change chords:

150

Study these harmonizations and say which you prefer. Decide also whether the modulation to the dominant or that to the relative minor of the dominant is the more suitable in the second phrase.

In the next question too a variety of harmonizations are possible.
'Complete the following fragment from a motet by Tye for SATB.'

The opening phrase can either remain in the tonic key, or modulate to the dominant.

Both the last three notes of bar 1 and the first three notes of bar 3 suggest either (a) the Interrupted Cadence, (b) the first inversion of the diminished triad, VII6, (c) the 'rising seventh', V_3^4, or (d) the 'passing $^6_4$', V_4^6.

Analyse these progressions:

Complete the alto and tenor parts, and also the chord indications:

V   VII⁶   V⁴₃   ⁶₄   VII⁶   V⁴₃   V⁶₄

Harmonize these few notes in several different ways:

Harmonize the whole of the given fragment in at least two different ways.

Additional exercises
Complete for SATB. Add suitable indications of tempi and dynamics.

Free Counterpoint in Two Parts

Study the sections on two-part writing in Books I and II. Here we emphasize two essentials:
   1. Look for satisfactory points of imitation, but never force an exact canon at the expense of good harmony.
   2. Let the parts be rhythmically independent and let there be overlapping of phrases.
   Consider this question:
'Complete the following, based on an extract from César Franck, to make two contrapuntal parts for soprano and bass:'

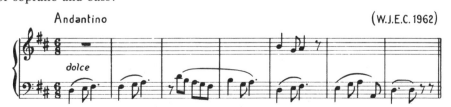

The rest in bar 1 and the soprano notes in bar 5 give a broad hint that a canon at the 8ve is expected. The quaver rest in bar 5, however, suggests that there the canon ends and the parts are free.

If, after experimenting with several openings, you cannot find a suitable imitation, write a free part that develops a motif of its own.

What is quite unforgivable is to harmonize note-for-note.

Write at least two solutions to each of these next questions. Remember to indicate tempi and dynamics.

'Complete the following to make two contrapuntal parts for soprano and bass:'

(W.J.E.C. 1960)

'Complete the following to make two contrapuntal parts for soprano and bass:'

(W.J.E.C. 1961)

'Either, Write a descant above this Northumberland folk-song (do not reproduce the words).'

(W.J.E.C. 1963)

Hev ye seen owt o'   maa bon-ny lad, And are ye sure he's   weel oh? He's

153

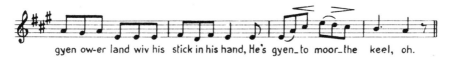

gyen ow-er land wiv his stick in his hand, He's gyen_to moor_the keel, oh.

'Or, Add a bass part to the melody (again, do not reproduce the words).'

Melody Writing

Little difficulty in writing 'a balanced melody of 16 bars' should be experienced by students who have practised the vocal and instrumental improvisation advocated in earlier chapters.

In an elementary examination a simple structure, such as AABA (cf. 'Down by the Sally Gardens') or ABBA (cf. 'The Lincolnshire Poacher') should be obvious. The 'A' phrases need not begin in exactly the same way, but their derivation must be clear.

Unless the rubric specifies a different procedure:

1. The first phrase remains in the tonic key (ending with an implied Imperfect or Surprise Cadence).
2. The second phrase modulates to the dominant ending with an implied Perfect Cadence.
3. The third phrase returns to the tonic or visits the relative minor (or relative major if the tonic key is minor).
4. The last phrase recapitulates in the tonic key. The final cadence may, if desired, correspond with the cadence figure at the end of the second phrase, i.e. it may be a transposition of the latter cadence figure into the tonic.

Following such precise instructions we must emphasize that the purely mechanical approach is ill-advised. Even within the limitations of this kind of question there is room for spontaneity and charm combined with good craftsmanship. Of the hundreds of good answers submitted each year we have yet to notice two that are exactly alike.

The four openings that follow are each to be continued to make balanced melodies of 16 bars. Every pupil should sing his melodies to the class.

For further practice (1) choose openings given in Book I, (2) utilize first phrases of folk and composed melodies, (3) improvise in various styles of your own invention.

THE GENERAL CERTIFICATE OF EDUCATION
ADVANCED LEVEL

Harmony in Four Parts

Study the given part carefully. It will usually contain rhythmic and melodic motifs from which your added parts may take shape. Consider the following bass part:

Rhythmic ideas:

(a)   (b)   (c)   (d)

Melodic ideas:
(e)   (f)

Here are four harmonizations of the bass in which these various ideas are employed.

1. (b) and (e) predominate. Notice the prevalence of step-wise movement.

2. (d) provides the opening idea.

Examine the soprano part. How would you explain the significance of bars 5–8?

3. A more vigorous setting arising from the use of (c).

4. The various motifs in combination.

In the paper from which this bass part is taken the question reads: 'In simple style add a soprano melody and parts for alto and tenor to the following bass.'

Notice the importance that is attached to the need for a soprano 'melody'. Notice too, the word 'simple'. A simple harmonization which is stylish and pointed is much to be preferred to a busy, pretentious texture where the parts move aimlessly and the harmonic framework is weak and ungainly.

Two-Part Contrapuntal Writing

'Add a cello part to the following violin melody. Insert bowing marks.'

156

Consider the following working:

Here we have an effective bass; it marches along in typical baroque style. But it is harmonic rather than contrapuntal, and suggests the orchestra rather than a chamber duo. The type of question under discussion is designed to test the candidate's ability to write a conversation-piece between two instruments in which the thematic material will be shared to some extent, and this implies rhythmic independence and a certain amount of imitation.

Consider the following version:

Points to notice:
There is some imitation. This could have been made more pointed by the use of rests in the cello part, but in view of the 'minuetto' nature of the given part it was decided to keep up the bass movement.

Phrases overlap (consider particularly bars 9–17). The instruments are on equal terms.

Melodic Writing

The candidate is asked to complete a melody in a given dance form and to provide a simple accompaniment.

This is a searching test of musicianship, since not only is the candidate's power of melodic invention called for, but also his ability to move freely and convincingly between the five most closely-related keys. Familiarity with binary form and the movements of the Suite is also implicit in the requirements. (See Chapter V)

Consider the following question:
'Complete the melody of the following Gigue for violin and add a simple accompaniment, in the style of the opening phrase, *either* for piano *or* for second violin, viola and cello. You may work in short score. Insert bowing or phrase marks.

The first section should total 8 bars and end in the relative major. The second section should be ten or more bars in length and include at least one further modulation before concluding in the tonic key. Do not copy out the given passage.'

Although time is of the essence in examinations, do not begin to complete the melody until you have taken your bearings. Think of the five closely-related keys, in this case:

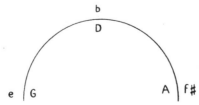

Examine the given passage carefully and sense the underlying harmonic framework and harmonic rhythm that lie behind the subsidiary harmony notes, passing notes, auxiliary notes, appoggiaturas, etc.:

You may then find it helpful to jot down the outlines of a musical sentence that continues in the same style, remembering to modulate to the relative major at the end of the first section (bar 8), and to include a further modulation in the second section.

Musical Sentences

We are not suggesting that you should strictly adhere to a preconceived ground-plan when composing your Gigue. You will find that in the act of composing one turn of phrase will give rise to the next, the form will grow out of the nature of the material to some extent. Nevertheless, it is helpful to have a sentence at the back of one's mind which will help to ensure that the music does not wander away into keys that are inappropriate in this type of movement.

Do not attempt more modulation than seems natural.

Remember that this is a test of melodic writing and contrive to get shapely phrases and a climax.

Remember too, that you are writing for instruments and are not confined within the limits of vocal range.

Here are two solutions, one for piano, and one in open score:

Now compose your own version using the instrumentation specified in the question.

1. 'Harmonize the following soprano melody by adding simple parts for alto, tenor and bass.'

2. 'Complete the following for two violins and cello. Work in open score, and insert bowing marks.'

3. 'Add a part for cello to the following passage for violin. Insert bowing marks.'

4. 'Add a violin part to the following and insert bowing marks.'

5. 'Complete the melody of the following Gavotte for violin and add a simple accompaniment, in the style of the opening phrase, either for piano or for second violin, viola and cello. Work in open or short score. Insert bowing or phrase marks.

The first section should total four bars and end in the relative major. (Note that the cadence will be at the half bar.) The second section should be eight (or more) bars in length and include at least one modulation before concluding in the tonic minor.

Do not copy out the given passage.'

6. 'Complete the following Minuet for string quartet. The dance must be in binary form, and the recommended length is 8 bars for the first section and 10 bars for the second. You may write in short or open score. Add bowing and dynamic marks.'

DIPLOMAS

Next we consider questions set by Trinity College of Music, London, in the Musical Knowledge examination. This is the General Paper which candidates for Practical Diplomas must pass.

'Complete the following in two parts.'

The key is B♭ and the closely-related keys are:

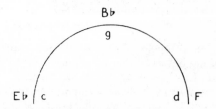

We notice a modulating sequence and several clearly defined motifs suitable for imitation. Consider this solution and then write one of your own:

'Complete the following for SAB.'

Upon singing and considering this melody we notice that:
  (i) three of the four phrases begin on the last beat of the bar. The third phrase, however, begins in the middle of the bar: some emphasis is needed here.
 (ii) the ♩. ♪ and ♩ ♫ rhythms are important.
(iii) the key is G and the closely-related keys are:

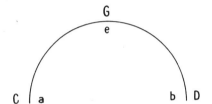

 (iv) the central and final cadences are similar.
  (v) since the quaver G is quitted by leap, it might be treated as a harmony note.
      It is difficult, however, to write interesting parts or to avoid repetitive harmonies and an exposed fifth, e.g.

A stronger progression is obtainable if we regard the E as an appoggiatura and the quaver G as a passing note.

 (vi) the second phrase passes through D and ends firmly in B minor, e.g.

(vii) the high, syncopated E may be treated as the dominant of A minor. We avoid returning prematurely to the tonic key by using the supertonic chromatic chord.

a: V⁶   I { a: I⁶
            { C: VI⁶ II#   V⁴₂   I⁶

Interest and tension may be increased by introducing continuous quaver movement by means of the changing note figure, suspensions, etc.

(viii) though the melody and rhythm of the second and fourth phrases are similar, the mood of the latter seems to be calm, e.g.

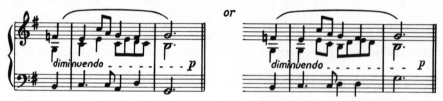

Consider the following treatment. Sing each part separately and in chorus.

Now close this book, write the melody from memory and compose a version of your own.

Harmonize the following extract in simple style by adding parts for Soprano, Alto, and Tenor:

(T.C.L. Dec. 1962)

On singing the given part we decide that:
  (i) rests and syncopations may give the necessary rhythmic interest without departing from the 'simple style' required.
  (ii) the dotted rhythms of bars 1, 2, and 4 might well be introduced subsequently.
  (iii) the key is F♯ minor and the closely-related keys are:

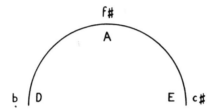

  (iv) the extract is not a complete musical sentence.
  (v) the first four bars may end in F♯ minor or modulate to A, e.g.

  (vi) there follows a modulating sequence and then a cadence which may be Imperfect in F♯ minor or Plagal in C♯ minor, e.g.

Decide which of the various alternatives are preferable and write a complete version of your own.

Two-Part Writing

'Complete the following by adding another flowing part. Indicate a suitable speed and add phrasing to both parts:

5. (T.C.L. July 1962)

6. (T.C.L. July 1963)

7. Allegro leggiero (T.C.L. April 1963)

8. Allegretto (T.C.L. Dec. 1962)

Three-Part Writing

'Complete the following for SAB.'

9.

'Harmonize the following melody by adding three parts in a simple style:'

10.

'Complete the following by adding two parts, one for Alto and one for Bass.'

11.

Four-Part Writing

'Add parts for Alto, Tenor, and Bass to the given melody:'

170

We conclude with harmony questions taken from **LRAM** General Musicianship examination papers.

'Harmonize this Bass in four parts:'

'Add a Tenor part below:'

'Insert a suitable position of a Dominant Seventh at each asterisk:'

3.

'Add three parts below the following Saraband:'

1.   (L.R.A.M. April 1963)

'Add a Bass below the following, entirely in Quavers excepting the last bar which should be a Minim:'

2.

'Write the Scale of B Major, descending, in a Compound Duple Time, and harmonize it in four parts. Add Key-signature and Bar-lines:'

3.

172

'Add three parts above this Bass (to make four parts in all).'

1.
Allegretto

'Add a Bass part to this Alto. Maintain crotchet movement except for the last bar.'

2.
Allegro

'Write chords at the asterisks to form the required cadences.'

3.

Plagal   Imperfect   Interrupted